a small fish.....
from the Philippines to the United Kingdom

ging aurelio laforteza

Copyright © 2022 Ging Aurelio Laforteza

ISBN: 9798362876043

All rights reserved, including the right to reproduce this book, or portions thereof in any form. No part of this text may be reproduced, transmitted, downloaded, decompiled, reverse engineered, or stored, in any form or introduced into any information storage and retrieval system, in any form or by any means, whether electronic or mechanical without the express written permission of the author.

Ging's incredible journey spanned across four cultures in three continents which transformed her from a naive third-world creature to someone who lives in more than one world at the same time.

As a child in the Philippines, she was always curious about the "peculiar" things in far-away lands across seas. A couple of decades later, she got married to a Brit and moved to this fairy-tale nation called the United Kingdom.

Suddenly, cultural differences became real and everything became abnormal. The familiar life she knew vanished, her beliefs questioned and her world of truths became false. Her day-to-day life was sometimes unbearable - all because she lived in a foreign country.

Determined to crush the barriers of her new world, Ging embarked on an extraordinary exploration to understand the new culture she is in and to understand her new self in her new world. Years later, Ging is happy at home….. in the United Kingdom.

Let this book accompany you through your own new worlds.....

Dedication

To my husband, parents, sisters, brother and in-laws,
'I love you!'

Thanks

To Araceli, Chen Chang, GLH, Jeff, Liz Felstead,
Lourdes Faustino Laforteza, Margie Deza Luistro, Rameses Aurelio,
Raymund Sison, Sam Nang Huoy, to my husband and
to other friends who gave me feedback,
'BIG thanks!'

To Chen Chang, Lourdes Faustino Laforteza, Margie Deza Luistro,
GLH, and to other contributors,
'BIG thanks!'

My dear Liz,

Thanks again for your BIG help. I am so privileged to have you on this journey.

Hugs,

Ging Li

Table of contents

1: Introduction 1

What this book is about
What this book is not about

2: My first world 3

My home country
Myself

3: A day like no other 7

Interlude 1.......... *9*

4: Weird, funny and outrageous 10

Gifts
Excuse me
Umbrellas
Attractive lady?
Bra-less
Where are the malls?
Anything goes
Let it snow, let it snow, let it snow
Finger-licking good
100 miles per hour
Hold the bloody doors
Oh, the smell!
Legs spread open
'Sir, my change please?'

5: They're not funny 20

UK size 6
Everything about food
Sorry, my friend
The mighty sun
Oh dear dandelion!
What shall we talk about?
Friends, where art thou?
Weird, funny and outrageous – no more
Corner store 2.0

6: Get me out of here 29

Language
Do what the Romans do
Colonial mentality + hierarchy culture
A matter of perspective

7: Dark moments 39

Was it just me?
Marriage
Masked façade

8: What I did 42

Nothing
Familiarise, familiarise, familiarise
Change habits
Accept the consequences and rewards
Avoid avoiding practicalities
Express myself
I am who I am
Marriage

Interlude 2.......... 51

9: The same, no more 52

Hold (not!) the bloody door
Beauty queens and kings
Excuse my new manners
How could I have forgotten?
100 miles an hour
We're a family
Kili-kili power
Too hot

10: No thanks 57

Food
Idiotic rules
Filipino time
Ships from my window
Spaghetti traffic
Measure of success

11: Not for me anymore 63

I know no one
Discipline, where art thou?
My house is OK
Blatant corruptions
What's in a name?
False helplessness
Just minding my own business

12: My great rewards 73

Multiple perspectives
Personal growth
Losing vs gaining identity

13: My take on this 80

14: epilogue: a small fish 82

Appendix.......... 83

Our cleaner drove a Mercedes Benz
I pointed with my mouth
Narrow panties please
No nice hats for me
Chip and Dale
More preservatifs please

I am not an Athenian or a Greek, but a citizen of the world.

— Socrates

1: Introduction

My journey began in the Philippines and continued on to the United Kingdom, to Australia and to Germany, before I returned once more to the United Kingdom. I want to share my experiences of living in those four different cultures in three different continents and how they have transformed me – for the better, I hope!

I have also been to twenty-three other countries and had a taster of their cultures. Holidaying in a country is hugely insignificant compared with living in a country if you want to truly understand the culture. However, none of my holidays failed to contribute to my education or change my views about life.

The experiences, both bad and good, that I gained from hopping from one culture to another inspired me to want to write a series of books. They will appeal to those who are interested in reading about other people's transformations through immersion in different cultures, and to those who would want to have an idea of how other people adapt and how long it can take.

What this book is about

This is my first book and it will focus on my first move, i.e., from the Philippines to the United Kingdom. Being my first, this transition dwarfed all of my other moves and it was the catalyst to my mind re-set.

This is a record of some of my discoveries, excitements, difficulties, joys and pains as I adjusted from Philippine culture to British culture. Most importantly, this is an account of my transformations and my changing views in life. Everything that I say here is based on my personal experiences, which may differ substantially from those of others. I hope that anyone reading this book will be inspired to take on a similar journey to widen their horizon through the understanding of different cultures. By doing so, I guarantee that you will change, sometimes in ways that you would never have thought possible. The value I derived far outweighs the difficulties I encountered along the way. This book is my celebration of that privilege.

Within the context of my journey, I encountered some difficulties during my adjustment period. Uprooting oneself and transplanting into a different culture can be daunting. For some, it might take only a few years to settle, but for others it might take forever, or it might not happen at all. My adjustment period was difficult and spanned a number of years. If you are in a similar situation, I hope that this book will offer you reassurance that your experiences are not unique. The dark moments will pass over time if you let them, as they did in my case. If you are still considering whether to move, I hope that you find my experiences worthy of reflection before your journey overseas, near or far. Adjusting your mindset appropriately prior to your move will make a difference. This book is my wish that you, too, will find incredible rewards in your journey, as I did in mine.

What this book is not about

This book is not about how to make someone's move to another country easy. I do not have qualifications on that topic, nor have I any education or training in psychology. Hence, this book must not be viewed as a source of advice on how to achieve a happy life on foreign soil.

2: My first world

My home country

Philippines has a tropical climate with high temperatures, high humidity and abundant rainfall. Average temperatures range from 25.5C to 28.3C but it is usual for temperatures to reach the low-to-mid thirties in the warmer months. High temperatures, coupled with high humidity, can make life very uncomfortable from March to May. Philippines has only two seasons: the dry season and wet season.

It was a colony of Spain for more than 300 years and was liberated by the Americans from Japanese colonisation later. This is why you can see Spanish influence in Filipino philosophies and thinking, and American influences in current Filipino lifestyles. The Filipino psyche of today is still heavily influenced by a colonial mentality where everything imported is considered superior.

Philippines is a very religious and relatively conservative country. In 2015, approximately seventy-five per cent of adults were Christians. Although very American on the surface, Catholicism implanted by the Spanish colonisers continues to dominate the current-day beliefs and practices.

Family ties are strong, hence the belief that 'blood is thicker than water'. Although it varies from one family to another, this belief applies also to extended family members (aunts, uncles, cousins) and also to more distant relatives. The concept of losing face is also quite strong and can sometimes become more challenging when the scenario concerns extended or distant family members.

Philippines is classed as a developing or a third-world country. It has a highly-marginalised society where a very few wealthy families control everything and a huge proportion of its population lives in poverty. Middle-class families live comfortably. They can afford the basics in life and have some spare cash for luxuries. During my time, most of the middle-class families could not afford international travel but they could afford the services of helpers. In this economically challenged country, prestige matters a lot so status symbols are very important.

Professional rank and material wealth are the widely-accepted indicators of one's success.

Myself

I was born in Iloilo City, the capital of Iloilo province, to a middle-class family. My father was a seaman and spent, on average, nine months of the year hopping from one port to another around the world. It is not unusual for fathers and/or mothers in the Philippines to live away from their families because of work. My mother was a full-time Mum who lovingly raised her children in a traditional Filipino way. I was the youngest of four siblings. I have a very loving family and I grew up in a home full of love and care.

I spent my childhood and teen life in my home town. My earliest realisation of faraway lands was when I was about five years old. My father came home one year and gave me a koala-bank (as opposed to a piggy-bank). I did not understand then why I had not seen such a funny-looking creature before, and why I would not be able to see one for real unless I went to Australia. I was told that I would have to ride a plane to see this faraway land and that I might be able to go there one day when I grew up.

Although I had never been outside of my country, I had awareness of 'other worlds' through the *National Geographic* magazines that my father brought with him every time he came back home. I remember seeing pictures of cacti in Arizona and thinking how alien looking those thorns were. I saw igloos and wondered why people would live like turtles. I saw the skyscrapers of New York and wondered whether I would ever have the chance to go to the USA. I saw people with white and black skins, which made me aware that I have a skin colour somewhere in the middle. Filipinos have black hair and seeing other people with blond hair really puzzled me.

At an early age, my parents taught me that the best way to improve my life would be through education. I excelled academically in elementary and high school, and was elected leader of our high school student council. I engaged in many extracurricular activities, such as Girl Scouts, where I formed many friendships with students from other schools and provinces. I worked very hard to secure a scholarship at one of the top three universities in the country and I left my hometown when I was sixteen to study in the capital city of Manila. That was the first time that I had lived away from my family. I would say that back then, it was unusual for a child to leave home before marriage. I was also taught by society that the second-best way to improve one's life is to leave Philippines and settle where the pastures are greener.

Driven by the idea that IT would boost my prospects, I completed a computing degree at De La Salle University (DLSU), which in my humble opinion, offered the best IT qualification in the country at that time. American English was the medium of teaching in DLSU and in all other schools and universities in the Philippines. DLSU students generally speak and write very good, if not excellent, English; possibly better than many Brits, in fact.

Apart from the excellent quality of its education, DLSU also has the reputation of being the university of choice for students from the country's millionaire families. As a consequence, learning how to adjust with Filipinos from wealthy backgrounds very different to mine became part of my academic education. It was challenging but it was a privilege as it opened my eyes to a different set of views based on financial demographics, and not on geography.

A few months after I graduated, I took up a teaching role in DLSU. It was a happy environment as I was paid very well by a rich employer and was offered many professional growth opportunities. During the time I was teaching there, DLSU was engaged in a seven-year collaboration with the UK's University of Brighton (UoB). During that collaboration, the computing departments of the two universities exchanged lecturers. DLSU sent its lecturers to UoB to complete either a master's degree or doctorate, while UoB sent its lecturers to DLSU to teach on DLSU's graduate programme. On the seventh and last year of collaboration, UoB sent their last lecturer to teach at DLSU. As a normal young Filipino lady, I dreamt of marrying a Filipino. My brown knight did not come but on that one fine unexpected day, a white man from the UK did!

Fast forward to 1994, my fiancé suggested that I spend Christmas in the UK to meet his family and to find out whether I'd be happy to live in his country. Being young and blinded by love, I did not really think much about his suggestion. I agreed without thinking much because at that time, the only important thing to me was that I was going to be with him over Christmas.

I did spend my Christmas that year in the UK and had a wonderful time. While in the country, I totally forgot the main reason for being there. I merely enjoyed my time with the man I love and in a place where I had never been before. At the end of that holiday, again without thinking seriously, I agreed to the plan to live in the UK permanently. Now a smarter lady, I believe that that was one of the most stupid things I ever did. I did not give my move the serious thinking it deserved. Looking back, I consider myself lucky that things turned out well in the end. Phew!

Five months after Christmas and aged twenty-four, I left Philippines without any serious thought of what my life in the UK would be like. All I knew was that, if things didn't turn out well, divorce was allowed in the UK. Though feeling sad, I did not have any hesitation in leaving my family and friends behind thinking that everyone had their own lives to make. It was in my DNA to welcome big changes so, young as I was, I did not have any hesitation or worry about what lay ahead. The only preparations I made were to resign from my job and to dispose of the few possessions I had as fast as I could.

3: A day like no other

My plane landed on 24 December 1994 at Heathrow Airport in the early hours of the morning. It was my first time outside of my home country and everything was so exciting. I was going to spend Christmas with my fiancé in his country.

After I had collected my luggage and on our way to the airport car park, I was surprised to see white puffs coming out of my mouth. I was seeing my first winter breath! Coming from a tropical country, I was in awe. It was super cool, just like in the movies. I knew then that I would have an exciting day ahead.

On our drive going out of the airport, my fiancé stopped at an intersection to give way to another car. The driver of the other car gestured for us to proceed and I was so impressed. I thought, *Oh my, how courteous British drivers are!* If you have experienced Philippine traffic, you will understand why this particular experience made such an impression on me. On a daily basis, motorists and commuters in the Philippines can easily spend two to three hours in a traffic jam travelling to a destination that might be just thirty minutes' drive away, if only drivers observed traffic rules.

I remember touring Brighton that day to distribute Christmas cards and being introduced by my fiancé to his family and friends. Thankfully, I was coping well with the UK winter due to my gigantic, astronaut-like outfit that probably weighed as much as I did. As we hopped from one place to another, I saw many fair-skinned people with different hair and eye colours. It was weird looking at people with pink or green or blue hair behaving so normally. The houses were so old and they all looked the same, the trees were without leaves, and it was dark at four o'clock in the afternoon. The reality was exactly the same as the worlds I had seen portrayed in books and in movies, though more interesting than anything words or images could convey.

Our last stop that day was dinner at a pizzeria in the town centre. As we waited for our pizzas to arrive, I suddenly felt very sleepy. I had heard about jet lag but had never really understood what it meant. I finally knew what it was about when my pizza arrived. The last thing I remembered that day was seeing the largest pizza I had ever seen in my life, with black olives scattered all over it. Then came zzzzzzzzzzzzzzz and my head was over my pizza!

I will never forget my first day outside of the Philippines. Even the little things we take for granted in our familiar daily lives can be a source of joy or wonder for someone who has not lived through them before. Given that millions of people are experiencing their 'first days' right now, isn't that a wonderful thought? I still look back to that day from time to time, and I still truly appreciate that feeling of awe. Just like a child, that feeling always propels me to go out and explore. I just know I will never grow up.

Interlude 1

I moved to the UK and got married in 1995. Thirty-five people attended the wedding, including the bride and the groom. It was indeed a small wedding! In the Philippines, "a small wedding" usually means a minimum of one hundred people, excluding the bride and groom and their immediate families.

4: Weird, funny and outrageous

There was never a dull moment during my first year in my new country. Every day was discovery day and I loved it! I was like a child again constantly curious about everything; sometimes unsure about what to do and oftentimes enthusiastic to learn or try everything. I can list a few little, ordinary things, among many, that I found weird, funny, or outrageous at that time.

Gifts

Filipinos like giving and receiving big gifts. When we receive one, we do not open it in front of the giver, especially if there are other people around. It was not explained to me why but I can only guess that it is to avoid any embarrassment in case the receiver does not like the gift.

I had no idea that the norm in the UK was the opposite. People in the UK normally open their gifts in the presence of the givers. The exception, of course, is when people receive Christmas gifts; they open them on Christmas Day. So guess what I did the first time I received a gift in the UK? I did not open it immediately. On learning about the norm a few months after, I felt so embarrassed that I had unintentionally behaved rudely towards a friend. Oops!

Excuse me

In the Philippines, when you are about to pass between two people in conversation, there is no need to say 'excuse me'. Filipinos simply lower their heads, extend their arms downwards and stretch their hands like offering a handshake, before taking steps between the two people.

The above had been so well ingrained in me that shaking it off proved challenging. The first time I caught myself doing it in the UK was at work when I got into the lift and stepped in between two people talking. At first, I was not aware that I was doing it until I saw the wondering expressions of those two people. I noticed that they were staring at my hands. Their heads followed me as I moved into the lift, and they looked at me and then at my hands again. Only then did I realise that they had stopped talking and that I was doing the 'excuse me' hand signal. Imagine that scene. It looks funny, right?

I wanted the lift floor to open up and swallow me. When I returned their gaze, they immediately stared straight ahead and acted as though they were not interested in me. What followed seemed like an eternal silence as the three of us looked straight ahead in embarrassment. Also imagine that you are waiting for the lift and when the door finally opens, you see three people dressed in corporate suits – two tall Caucasian men either side of a short skinny Asian woman – all standing straight stiffly to attention and all looking red.

Umbrellas

Being in a hot country, Filipinos use umbrellas to shield them from the harmful rays of the sun. We don't differentiate umbrellas from parasols. In the UK, people only use umbrellas when it's raining.

I was walking happily to work one fine summer's day with my umbrella open. I was passing a car parked on the street when I heard a girl, perhaps five years old, asking politely why I was using an umbrella even though it was not raining. She was with her younger brother, who was perhaps four years old. It looked as though their adult companion(s) must have stopped momentarily to pick up something from the corner shop. To an adult in the UK, I must have looked strange. In these two children, I could see only confusion and bewilderment. I stopped for a short time and explained that apart from keeping one from getting wet, umbrellas can actually be very useful in protecting oneself from the sun. 'Oh, I see!' they said, with genuine child-like realisation. I saw from both their faces that their young, inquisitive minds were working. I smiled at them and they smiled back. *Nice, polite kids*, I thought.

I continued my walk and although I felt triumphant in introducing a foreign concept to two little Caucasian people, I could not help feeling that I was a strange person in this strange land. I knew I was a normal person, until I moved to the UK.

Attractive lady?

Do I have brown skin? Yes. Do I have long hair? Yes. Am I slim? Yes. Do I look attractive? No.

A stereotype for a beautiful woman in the Philippines is someone who is *mestiza* (Filipino blood mixed with a Caucasian race), has fair skin, and a long, thin, pointed nose. The whiter the skin, the more attractive a woman is. I certainly do not to belong to that group of women who make heads turn, who are asked for their phone numbers, and who are offered free drinks. I grew up believing that I looked acceptable and that, with a great make-up artist, I could look nice (at best), should the occasion arise. Although on certain occasions I wish I was beautiful, I am certainly comfortable most of the time that I am not.

I knew that my assessment of my physical appearance was fair until a colleague of mine, who knew I was married, asked me for a date. There were a few others who also asked. Also while on holiday in France, a couple of well-toned, good-looking guys kept staring at me while I was having a quick rinse under an outdoor shower on the beach in Monaco. I was oblivious to the stares but my husband told me. On many occasions, my husband also received comments from friends and colleagues about his beautiful wife. While attending a New Year's Eve ball at Vienna's Royal Palace, a distinguished-looking man asked my husband if he could take a photo of me. He also invited us to sit at his table with his distinguished-looking friends.

Suddenly, the brown skin that I would have given up for a fairer one became my asset; the flat wide nose I have no longer mattered, and the non-mestiza features I have were no longer a drawback. The truth that I had believed for more than twenty years no longer appeared to be true. I could not believe my luck. Fate sometimes works in my favour.

Bra-less

Philippines is a very religious and conservative country. When I was still living there, there was a stigma attached to ladies going bra-less. It was actually quite unfortunate because in a hot country, wearing a bra could feel like a punishment.

In contrast, the UK is considerably cooler than in the Philippines. However, it can sometimes feel more uncomfortable because unlike in the Philippines, air-conditioning is not widely used. The abundance of heritage properties, combined with only a few hot days in the year, does not incentivise the people to spend money on cooling systems. Therefore during the few very hot summer days, it is very tempting not to wear a bra.

I often complained about this discomfort to my husband and he kept on trying to convince me not to wear a bra if it was not comfortable. Being very Filipino still, I quickly dismissed his idea by saying that I could not not wear a bra because people would look at my nipples; to which my husband simply said, 'So what?'

It took me a long time to gather my nerves and give in to the 'so what' attitude. One day, I finally got the courage and went out of our house without my loyal bra. I felt very self-conscious at first and very paranoid that everyone was looking at my nipples. However, the feeling of air and the freedom of movement were very liberating. In case you are wondering – yes, I noticed that some people stared at my nipples but hey, 'So what?'

Where are the malls?

One of the famous pastimes in the Philippines is going to shopping malls. It is not surprising then that the malls in the Philippines dwarf the malls in the UK. The former can be described as resorts by UK standards. Apart from shops, a mall can have recreation centres (multi-screen cinemas, bowling alleys, theatres, skiing arenas, ball parks, etc), rows of indoor/outdoor restaurants, museums, galleries, churches, gardens, beauty and health centres, etc. These malls open every day usually from 10:00a.m. to 8:00p.m. except during the Christmas season when many of them open from 10:00a.m. to 10:00p.m.

When I arrived in the UK, I found it odd that there were not many malls in towns and cities smaller than London, and that they were miniscule compared with the malls in the Philippines. The retail stores were usually open from nine to five, Mondays to Saturdays only, including the grocery stores. I was totally surprised by that because the UK is one of the most progressive countries in the world and yet, in this respect, I felt like time had gone back to my mother's younger years in the Philippines. Some said that people needed to rest and not work all the time, so UK malls were closed on Sundays. Although that is true, I could not be persuaded because surely, many of the unemployed people would have welcomed the opportunity to be offered jobs on weekends and rest on some weekdays. Perhaps a Brit won't understand but I thought it was really strange.

Anything goes

I lived in Brighton during my first year in the UK. Brighton was a town (now a city) where anything goes. Pink hair? Grubby tangled hair? Torn tights? Two men or two women kissing on the streets? Rings attached to noses? Tattoos? Topless on the beach? Different shoe on each foot? Anything you can imagine was there. It was bizarre. I was Alice in *Alice in Wonderland* in a world of abnormalities. It was entertaining.

Brighton is also famous for emerging artists who wish to explore new and different visual art styles. They often express their thoughts and talents through street art, and tourists come to see them. Regarding performing arts, there is no shortage of artists in Brighton. There are buskers every day who add a buzz to the place, and who constantly explore and introduce new talents.

It took me a while to understand that street performers are not beggars. Some of them do it to gain exposure or training, while for others, busking is their livelihood. In the Philippines, artists would be extremely embarrassed to perform on the street. It also took me a while to understand why some graffiti would attract tourists. Back in my first world, graffiti is considered tatty and seedy.

Let it snow, let it snow, let it snow

A white Christmas is beautiful!

I will never forget my first experience of snowfall. I was working in an office with a floor-to-ceiling glass wall that I shared with another lady. I was the only person in the room that day. I was going about my routine tasks when suddenly, something extraordinary happened – snowflakes started to fall. I was completely mesmerised. Perhaps ten minutes passed before I realised I was merely staring at the sky.

I grabbed my jacket and went out to feel the snowflakes on my face. I was a girl again, playing outside of my workplace, and I didn't care. My lady boss was fascinated by my reaction and told me to take my time and savour every moment of it.

Seeing snowfall for the first time was truly magical to me. I had only seen it in movies, or in photos of friends and family, or in magazines. Whenever I look back to that day, I feel so privileged. I can still taste the first flake of snow that fell on my lips.

Finger-licking good

My parents' instructions not to lick stamps carried the same importance as toilet training, as did not to lick my fingers when turning over the pages of a book, and certainly not to lick fingers after handling currency notes. To do so would mean spreading germs and viruses to other people. I am 200 per cent certain that other Filipino children are taught the same. Licking anything in public is not normal in my home country. It is considered unhygienic and bad manners.

I was also taught to eat bananas with their skins on and to peel one gradually as I eat the flesh. That way, I do not need to touch the flesh with my grubby hands unless, of course, I have washed my hands just before eating the banana.

In 1995, I found myself seeing all of the above in this land called England. I actually conducted a little study over a period of one week during my first year in the country. I counted the number of people who ate bananas with their peels on or off. According to my very scientific study (wink, wink!), about thirty per cent of people in the UK handled banana flesh with unwashed hands. Also, at that time, about twenty-five per cent of people in the UK handled their sandwiches with bare hands and licked their fingers after they had eaten even though they had not washed their hands.

Although not common, I also noticed that a few people working in smaller post offices licked the stamps before sticking them on envelopes. At that time, I also observed that it was quite common for people in the UK to lick the envelopes to seal them. Tell you what, I had never bought a letter opener in my life but I did when I learned about that! Worse, some staff members wetted their fingers with their tongues when they counted currency notes. When their fingers dried up, they would lick them again and continue on counting. I'm sure my grandmother would have fainted if she'd seen what I saw!

100 miles per hour

I am only 5ft 1in tall with short legs so most British women are taller than I am. Anatomically, when walking or running, I would arrive at a destination later than most British women would. When walking with a group, I would need to walk briskly even when everyone else is walking leisurely. Sometimes, I looked like one of those tiny wind-up dogs with their tiny legs working frantically in order to keep pace with their owners. Isn't that hilarious? Sometimes, my hubby would tug me so that I kept up with everyone.

Culturally, I walk more slowly than British people do. I attribute that to my home country being hot and humid. If not in shade, people there don't normally walk at all. If there's a shade, people usually walk slowly. The Brits, on the other hand, appeared to be constantly in a race. My guess at that time was, that the UK was a cold country and everyone wanted to get to his or her destination quickly. I found it funny and amusing to people-watch because the street scenes looked like time-lapse video clips.

Hold the bloody doors

In the UK, when people go through doors, they hold them open for the next person as a courtesy. The rationale being, that the door won't bang into the next person's face (and break their nose). I found that weird at first because, surely, it is common sense that the next person will stop the door if they see it about to bang into them. Why can't they stop the door themselves?

In the Philippines, you will sometimes see door-holding among groups of people who know each other or someone being gentlemanly holding a door for a woman if she is not several meters away from the door. In the UK, this is a general custom and people do wait for the next person, stranger or not, even if the next person is several metres away.

Like many other UK norms, I didn't know this at first. In fact, I had already been staying in the UK for a few weeks before I learned about it. I must have unknowingly annoyed many people before then. Luckily though, I hadn't flattened anyone's face or broken anyone's nose. Phew!

Oh, the smell!

My first summer in the UK was great. It was an adventure on its own as I discovered so many things about my new home. I discovered how hot the UK could get, and saw the beach covered with scantily clothed bodies and women going topless. My seaside city could become very crowded as people from the surrounding areas swarmed in, and I saw that the menus of restaurants changed to suit the season. The list goes on.

Unfortunately, I also discovered how smelly it can get! I was on a bus one day when suddenly, the air became foul. *I recognise that smell*, I thought. Someone on the bus had body odour. It was so bad that I retched! As the summer progressed, the body odour syndrome became more common not only on public transport but also in workplaces, in entertainment centres, shopping malls, in business locations and just about anywhere. What surprised me even more was the fact that even professionals, dressed in professional outfits, could be smelly and they were oblivious to the offence.

The UK is basically a cold country and for a large part of the year, people don't sweat. My guess was that, the body odour issue had not really surfaced in the national consciousness. In contrast, since Philippines is a hot country, body odour has become a national stigma. The embarrassment is significant enough for others to lose respect for the person who smells. Hence, it is important to maintain personal hygiene, especially in professional work environments, and even when the weather is scorching hot.

Experiencing summer smell in the UK made me appreciate and admire the skills of Filipinos in managing their body odours.

Legs spread open

I was raised in the Philippines at a time when girls were groomed to move with a feminine quality. Hence, it was not surprising that those girls grew up as poised women. Grandmothers, mothers, older sisters and even female teachers taught girls not to sit with their legs spread open, and were very strict about it. I definitely received at least a million stern looks from my grandmother for sitting with my legs open. As an innocent little girl, I didn't understand then why that bit down there had to be kept away from the party. ☺

I expected the UK to have something similar due to its history of queens and princesses. When I arrived in the country, I saw many legs spread open when sitting down, whether the person was wearing trousers or a skirt. Some were slightly open and some were wide-open. *Wow*, I thought, *this is a charming open place!*

'Sir, my change please?'

Our first time on public transport in Japan was embarrassing. In our first week in the country, we took a bus to buy groceries. Our friends had initially advised us to buy bus tickets for going around the city which were cheaper than paying cash. As we had not already bought our tickets, I decided to pay in cash. I pulled a crisp ten-dollar bill from my wallet and inserted it directly into the ticket machine. The driver looked at me and without hesitation, tapped the machine until my note went through. He then continued driving while I remained standing at the front waiting patiently. When we were almost at our stop, I looked at the driver and asked, 'Sir, my change please?' He looked at me half smiling and said, 'Excuse me?' A fellow passenger behind me said, 'You'll never get your change on the bus. Once you insert your bill in the machine, you never get it back.' My husband and I flew out of the bus in record time making sure not to glance back. We were so embarrassed!

Decades later, I was chatting casually about this with someone who offered a different perspective to our experience. In the Philippines, there is a term *promdi*, meaning 'from the country' or parochial. It is a derogatory expression. Although everyone has their own story of not knowing what to do in unfamiliar situations, everyone's too embarrassed to make it obvious to others because of the stigma of being branded as a *promdi*. I am now aware that however embarrassing our experience may have been to us at that time, it would not be considered embarrassing in many cultures. Us standing at the front of the bus and waiting for the change would not have caused people from other cultures to think that we were *promdis*. Some people would have only thought that we were foreigners and that we didn't know how things operated in a foreign country. Some of them might even have been reminded of their own similar experiences in other countries. On that basis, there was no reason at all for us to have felt embarrassed.

In summary, sometimes we feel embarrassed about what we say or do because we are making judgements based on the accepted norms of our home countries.

Lourdes Faustino Laforteza
Philippines to Canada

5: They're not funny

A year had passed since I'd moved and my honeymoon with the UK was over. The new wonders were no longer new or wonderful. Instead, they had been replaced by day-to-day irritations that became heavier to bear with each passing month. I had definitely experienced many of those irritants from day one but they did not enter my consciousness until some time later. Either, their effects on me earlier had been masked by the thrill of new discoveries, or their impact wasn't that noticeable until I had become exasperated by something else.

UK size 6

I was a size 6, bordering on size 5. Back in 1995, it was almost impossible to get clothes of my size in the UK. Women's clothing usually started from a size 10, although a few brands offered size 8. If a size 6 was available, it was usually more expensive than the larger sizes of the same brand and style. If I had chosen that option, I would have had to pay the higher price for the size 6 and for alterations as well because some parts of the garment would still be too big for me. The alterations could be very expensive; sometimes as much as, or more than, the original item itself.

I bought my ordinary, everyday clothes from childrenswear departments. Although they were much cheaper, I always ended up wearing clothes that did not have a lady's shape. Work clothes were a nightmare because there weren't any suits in childrenswear. Almost always, I had to buy a size 8 and pay a fortune to alter the merchandise.

For years, I wore bras and knickers for girls with cute animal and/or floral prints. One day, I went to a lingerie section of a department store to get something worthy of my age. The sales assistant was really patient in trying to find me a pair of bra and knickers small enough. After she'd carried half the stock from the storeroom, she finally showed me a pair small enough. Unfortunately, it had cute, smiling yellow birds with eyelashes printed on it - the pair was for an 11-year-old girl.

For over a decade, every time I went back to the Philippines, I bought clothing supplies that would last me for five years. I would wear and bring worn-out clothes on the outward journey and on my return, I would leave the old clothes behind to make space for the new wardrobe in my luggage.

The constant disappointment over many years of coming home empty-handed from shopping left me extremely tired and very frustrated. Everything I wore depended on whatever little size 6 was available rather than on how I wanted to express and present myself. I felt like a fake and that I was living as someone else. One of my basic needs was not available to me and I was hungry for recognition that genuine small people like me exist. I was an outsider in my new world.

Everything about food

I remember one particular afternoon: it was my first time in one of the UK's biggest grocery stores. My eyes lit up when I saw how big the tomatoes were, how fat the eggplants were (or aubergines, as the Brits call them), and at the sight of other strange-looking produce. Every item had an expiry date too, which I thought was an excellent idea. Back in the Philippines, expiry date on food items was an alien concept. People might, at times, have sniffed at food instead to check whether it was still OK.

Sadly, I had issues with food during my adjustment years. In my first couple of years in the UK, I found British food bland and pretty unappetising. Fish dishes were tasteless if it were not for the creamy sauces that they were usually smeared with. Red meats tasted pretty much like cardboard, and vegetables were usually boiled or roasted giving them plain boring flavours.

'What do you mean, "drain the rice"? That is sacrilege!' I ate rice three times a day, 365 days a year in the first 24 years of my life, and rice was meant to be fluffy. It is cooked by letting the grains absorb the water and whatever excess there is, is left to evaporate. Unfortunately, someone who brought rice into the UK had a different idea. Brits boil their rice and once the grains are tender enough, they drain the water. Hence, the grains are not fluffy.

I was fed up with having to cope with boiled rice when eating out. On its own, this issue would not have caused me to feel upset. However, over a period of time, the cumulative dissatisfaction with what I had been eating caused me to question whether it had been the right decision to move to this country.

When I left my home country, I did not really think about the effects of not being able to eat Filipino food and ingredients. I was restless and I was always looking for something that was missing.

Sorry, my friend

How can one console a friend who has just had a miscarriage?

A good friend who is a non-Filipino immigrant, lost her baby. It was my first encounter with the grief of someone I'd got to know in the UK and I was unsure how to behave towards her. All I was sure about was that she needed to feel loved.

If my friend had been a Filipino, I would have chosen to spend some time with her. Filipinos are more open with their emotions and we generally prefer to have a shoulder to cry on. In contrast, I know that many Brits would prefer to be given some space and would rather not talk about their circumstances. I had no idea what the norm was in my friend's culture about losing a baby.

I went to see my friend a few days after I'd heard the news. On my way there, I bought some flowers hoping that they would make her feel better. I still did not know what to do as I rang the bell at her home. Her husband opened the door and I think I said something like, 'I'm sorry to hear your news and I've come to drop some flowers by for my friend. Her husband invited me in but I was so unsure that all I managed to say was something like, 'Thanks, but sadly, I can't stay long.' The husband called my friend and she met me at the door. I repeated what I'd said, hugged her, and looked at her for a few seconds hoping that some wisdom would come to me so I'd know what to do next. Unfortunately, all my wits abandoned me and I chose to leave instead of spending some moments with a very sad friend.

Whenever I remember that event, I feel regret. When I look back, my guess is that my friend would have wanted me to stay. Even now, I feel very bad that I left her, not because she may have wanted some space, but because I was so embarrassed that I didn't know what to do. I had nothing to base my decision upon. I wanted to be a friend but I was caught in this cultural void. I carried the guilt for some time after I saw her on that sunny, yet gloomy, day.

The mighty sun

Many Filipinos avoid direct sun. Some avoid it because they don't want to get sunburn; others dread the idea of becoming sweaty and smelly; many do not want to look darker; others do not want to feel the heat; and so on. As for me, I avoid the sun because I do not want to look darker. In my eyes, the fairer the skin, the more flexibility there is in what a lady can wear in terms of the colour of clothes and make-up. So I prefer fairer skin to darker skin. In contrast, British people love the sun. Given that the sun comes out only half of the year in the UK, I can understand the British people's craving for its warmth.

During UK summers, the beaches are usually full of scantily clad bodies, both male and female. I, on the other hand, will turn up with a wide-brimmed SPF50 hat, long sleeve SPF50 top, SPF50 trousers, socks, and a mile-thick facial sunblock that I top up every two hours or so. (I can see the grin on your face!) While British people sun-bathe, I try to find a space with as much shade as I can.

In spring, summer and autumn, it was common for my husband and me to walk on opposite sides of the road. Him on the sunny side, me on the...... (Guess which side I was on!)

I have brown skin and, unfortunately, I get much darker in a very short time. For that reason, I have stayed away from the sun since my teenage years. As a consequence, I have become prone to headaches whenever I am exposed to the sun for longer than approximately fifteen minutes. I never go away on holiday without paracetamol. Unfortunately, in previous workplaces, it was quite common for bonding activities to be outdoors. My choices were either to suffer a headache and become darker, or to be seen as socially challenged. Worse, some workstations in offices were next to windows in full sun. Where there was not much space available, it could be awkward to ask for my desk to be moved. It was especially awkward if I was just starting a new job.

In scenarios like the above, I felt that I was being forced to give up a part of me in order to earn my living. It was a clash I'd never had before and it was unsettling.

Oh dear dandelion!

Until I moved to the UK in my mid-twenties, I didn't need to clean our house, cook, wash or iron my clothes (not even my underwear!) as I had grown up with helpers in our household. I was also lucky to have parents who valued and respected human life no matter where people were in society. My siblings and I were taught to treat our helpers with dignity and to provide them with opportunities. My parents sent many of our helpers to schools so they could have better chances in life.

I also grew up hearing that life abroad was very challenging because you do everything yourself. Hence, it was not a surprise to me that my husband and I had to do all the household chores between us. In fact, I expected it. In practice, however, it was a difficult change in my life.

It was summer, and one late Sunday afternoon, I was pulling out dandelions from our back garden. I was told that these weeds grow very deep roots. Pulling their upper parts would not eradicate them so I needed to pull up their roots too if I didn't want them to keep on coming back. I did as I was told. I kept on digging the soil to completely remove the first dandelion I had laid eyes on. I kept on going for what seemed like forever. Then, suddenly, before I had pulled my first dandelion out completely, I burst into a sob – out of nowhere. I looked around our garden and saw many more dandelions, and then out burst a flood of emotions.

I was actually taken by surprise at my outburst. It seemed so silly to be crying over a dandelion. However, after I had mulled things over, I realised that it was not really the dandelions that I was crying about. It was a cry out of self-pity. I had not needed to do the gardening before. I was often tired from working five days a week and then I had to do the chores during evenings and weekends as well. My husband was excellent in sharing the chores. However, I was already battling with the everyday mental and emotional stress at work and in my private life. Any chores that I was not accustomed to were extra challenges that made all the other challenges even harder. I was physically, mentally and emotionally exhausted.

What shall we talk about?

A typical Filipino will talk openly about financial matters. It is not unusual to hear, 'If only I had money.....' or, 'When I have the money.....' somewhere in a Filipino social conversation. As you would expect, in my early years in the UK, I was quite outspoken about being happier if and when I had money.

I noticed that British people are a lot more private about their finances. I sensed the feeling of uneasiness creeping in whenever a social conversation touched closely on money. I had this impression that even expressing one's desire to become rich was uncomfortable to some whom, I suspect, formed negative perceptions of me.

I don't hold it against British people if they would rather not talk about money. I'm sure that there are topics British people would like to talk about that Filipinos would rather not. However, I found myself having to refrain from talking about topics that my native culture would consider as acceptable. My brain had to constantly think about things that I would not have a second thought about in my native culture. After a while, the constant sifting of thoughts became mentally draining to a point where I would rather not say anything. I was always concerned about what people would think of what I had said so I had no inner peace.

Friends, where art thou?

While growing up, British people in the Philippines have a reputation for being uptight. Unlike the many Americans in the country, the Brits were considered aloof, though not horrible.

I was so relieved when, during my first day in the country, I found my fiancé's family, friends and colleagues warm and welcoming. My parents-in-law treated me as if I were their daughter as soon as I met them. Minutes after I was introduced, I felt comfortable with my fiancé's siblings and their partners. I was also received warmly in my fiancé's friends' homes, and was treated by my fiancé's colleagues just like they treated others in their workplace.

Why then, did it take me a long time to establish friendships in the UK?

Mostly, everyone in my UK circle had jobs, just like mostly everyone in my Philippine circle. The significant difference was that, my circle in the Philippines had helpers while my circle in the UK had none. The latter were expected to do their own household chores. That, of course, reduced everyone's time in my UK circle to socialise.

I also found that people in the UK were more private. It's not a criticism but merely an observation. Unfortunately (though understandably), it took longer to bond with someone when the topics of discussion were mostly impersonal.

The British trait of being private, coupled with reduced time to socialise, is no one's fault but contributes to the difficulty for immigrants to penetrate the local circle and to integrate. This is not the only reason of course, but it does contribute to the difficulty.

I would say that I had a decent number of friends and acquaintances in the UK in my early years; most of them were my colleagues or my husband's colleagues. Sadly, I had no one who I really considered as a close friend. Hence, apart from my husband, I had no one to share my more personal stories with. I bottled up everything and I felt so lonely in a crowd.

Weird, funny and outrageous – no more

In the previous chapter, I listed a few things that I found weird, funny and outrageous during my early days in the UK. As time went by, they stopped being weird, funny and outrageous.

The subtleties of everyday interactions with people, in both my inner and outer circles, were supposed to excite me but instead, they became constant sources of embarrassment. My enjoyment in meeting people diminished.

Many of my preferences that were considered normal in the Philippines were seen as peculiar in the UK. Those peculiarities highlighted that I was different from the locals so I did not feel that I belonged.

The realisation that I am attractive to other people should have been a source of joy for me but instead, it was short-lived because I became unsure of who or what I was. My twentysomething perception of myself became blurry in my mind. I no longer knew myself very well.

I should have celebrated my newfound freedom to go bra-less but instead, I lost my grip on what's decent or not, what's normal or extraordinary, or what's good or bad. Without firm standards, I lost my sense of judgement and relied heavily on what my husband thought before I could make my own decisions. I was not rooted and I became dependent.

My appreciation of self-expression, e.g., pink hair, faded and was replaced by my contempt for anything that wasn't ordinary or elegant. The character of the place where I lived was not my style and the town appeared to me as tatty. Over time, the things that I saw and experienced every day choked me. I started to hate the things I did not hate before.

The thrill of snow ceased when, every year, I would fall on slippery icy roads. The thrills were replaced by fear and hatred because I had to put up with a fall every year. Every time I fell, the impact on me was not only physical but also mental and emotional. It was only a fall but somehow, it left me feeling so unequipped and less able to just move on with my life.

My cringy feeling when I saw people licking things turned into a strong dislike. I hated it when shop assistants licked their fingers before they loosened the opening of a plastic bag because I knew that I would be handling that bag. I easily got angry with shop assistants. I was not exactly known to friends in the Philippines as a patient person, but my patience got even shorter.

Looking back at those early years, I can now say that each issue was petty in the grand scheme of things. However, when those issues came together at the same time during my first few years in the UK, they drove me nuts. I was not in a healthy state. No one understood me; not even myself.

Corner store 2.0

I relocated to the UK from Taiwan, a tiny but super-packed island. Although it has now become my normality, I struggled at first with the shopping experience here in the UK.

In Taiwan, we have many (perhaps too many) 24/7 stores on almost every corner. They provide a wide variety of services that you would not believe – such talented staff! Aside from groceries, they sell hot food and drinks (like Costa), transport tickets (trains and coaches), and concert and performance tickets. Customers can also pay bills, taxes, and fines there; arrange for parcel deliveries faster than post offices can; and enjoy many other services in one stop. They also offer services at decent prices at any time of the day and on any day. Those shops are like compact shopping malls or consolidations of high-street stores.

In the UK, I find that each place has a sole purpose only. Hence, accomplishing one's tasks may require a couple of hours running around the town centre and must be done during daytime (not after 6:00p.m.). There were very many times when I needed to be super organised to do all my errands before everything closed. On a working day, I needed to plan my routes in advance to make it to places on time after work.

At the time of writing (8:00p.m. on a Sunday evening), I have this urge to go downstairs to get a takeaway 'tea egg' from a 7/11 store – like I always did in Taiwan!

Overall, my life in the UK is far from being horrible. I wouldn't still be here after five years otherwise. The best strategy for a foreigner is to make oneself like a sponge, i.e., you absorb everything around you. In the end, you will become almost like everyone else - and that was how I overcame my shopping difficulty in the UK.

Chen Chang
Taiwan to United Kingdom

6: Get me out of here

So far, the difficulties I've mentioned tended to be specific and, on their own, minor. They were obstacles that would not normally trip me up under my usual mental and emotional state because their effects would tend to be contained and easier to manage.

There were, however, other difficulties that had effects on multiple aspects of my life. I found them more difficult to address because either they required new knowledge and skills that could be attained only over time, or they required a change in the mindset that had been subconsciously ingrained in me for almost a quarter of a century. Sometimes, subconscious mentality is harder to reset than conscious mentality.

Language

Language skills are a must and greatly influence one's chances of becoming happy in another country. I had underestimated the power of my language skills – or lack of them. Before my move, I could speak and write English, and I thought that was enough.

Does grammar matter?

In the Philippines, writing and speaking correct English is a big deal. It can actually influence one's success or failure in a profession because the level of one's ability to write and speak English well is one of the yardsticks used when people decide either to mock or respect someone. There is some element of shame when someone speaks poor English. As a result, many Filipinos feel inferior to other Filipinos merely because of their inability to speak English.

I would say that my English grammar and vocabulary are of an acceptable standard. They are lower than this book's standard because I have asked my husband to correct my grammar and have asked a proofreader to check. Luckily, I found out early on that the Brits do not generally mind if one's grammar is terrible as long as they can understand what that person is saying. They are aware that many Brits cannot speak English correctly so why would they expect non-Brits to have perfect English grammar? Besides, most Brits cannot speak my language at all so, from their point of view, I can already do more than they can.

Socially, it didn't really bother me much that I could not speak correct English. Unluckily, that was not true professionally. In my early UK days, I did not want to have a job that required a lot of dedication as I was still adjusting to my move and also to married life. Hence, I worked part-time as an administrative assistant at a university; a job which only required some amount of thinking from nine to five a few days a week. A small part of my job required writing reports and disseminating information via written channels. It required some level of grammatical skills which caused me some degree of stress. Since my job was very far from the high end of the pay scale, my stress level was not really significant.

As I adjusted to my home environment, I took a master's degree in computing to update my knowledge and skills, and resumed my career as a full-time IT Business and Systems Analyst. As a computing professional and earning more than in my previous job, I was expected to deliver a more professional service. On one hand, writing my deliverables became easier because a large proportion of the documents I produced were technical documents that used IT notations. On the other hand, the small proportion of my deliverables to which IT notations do not apply had to be written in English at a professional standard. I became more stressed. Apart from using my brain to do things necessary for my job, I also needed to make more effort in constructing my sentences – more than would a native English-speaking person. At the end of each working week, I was mentally exhausted.

Not fast enough

My concern about my grammar was actually less severe than my concern about my brain's ability to process what I heard. I did very well in school, and I finished two undergraduate degrees and one master's degree. Therefore, I am confident that my brain is above average. However, when it comes to language, my brain just isn't switched on.

When I tried to be mindful of what was going on, I realised that English words were going in through my ears and they were being received by my brain as streams of English words. They were then being processed and converted into my own native language, and only then could I understand what was said. A similar process happened every time I said something; only in reverse and with an additional step. I formulated my message in my brain in my own language, my brain converted the words into English, and I then needed to think about the English sentence construction. Only then was I able to say what I needed or wanted to say. The process sounds logical but it was as inefficient as it was time-consuming. In reality, it was not effective.

My duties as an IT Business/Systems Analyst included facilitating workshops and attending meetings with clients and technical teams. I was fine with one-to-one interactions or even one-to-two, but I always dreaded having group conversations, especially formal ones such as workshops and big group meetings. I struggled to understand discussions because by the time my brain had processed the first sentence of what a person had said, that person had already said their second sentence. By the time I'd processed the second sentence, the discussion would already have moved on to another person or perhaps to a few other people.

From a communication point of view, it was very frustrating. From a livelihood point of view, it was extremely stressful holding on to a well-paid professional job in a corporate environment while struggling with communication problems. I felt very unequipped for my job which affected my performance at work significantly. Not only did I feel that I was working to a lower standard than I would have been if language had not been a barrier, but I also had difficulty pushing my career to a higher level. I saw a few colleagues moved on higher up the corporate ladder faster than I did, yet I knew that I was brighter and more capable than they were in all other aspects. Those times were like slaps in the face. I did recognise, however, that I had a language disability that I needed to overcome. I did not blame anyone but myself, and my self-belief shrank considerably.

And the winner is . . .

At no time were my lack of language skills more frustrating than when I needed to argue with my husband, or to engage in a debate with my colleagues, or to present an opposing idea to anyone. It was extremely difficult listening to the other party, translating words, understanding what they said, formulating my counter-arguments in Filipino, translating the words into English, constructing the sentences and then finally saying what I needed to say. Most of the time, I was not able to express myself as clearly and as thoroughly as I wanted to because some steps in that long-winded process were lost in my brain as I attempted to do everything at speed. This inadequacy often resulted either in me losing my argument, or the discussion not progressing as well as both parties had wanted it to.

Imagine the above happening to you over a long period of time. For me, the first emotion that usually kicked in was frustration, then defeat, followed by anger, then loneliness, then the feeling of being lost, and then sadness.

Mind my language

If my grammar and vocabulary weren't bad enough, my knowledge about appropriate slangs and terminologies was worse. I came from an area in the Philippines where sometimes, we would use the term *breed* in describing a person with certain characteristics. For example, it is fine to say that 'She came from a breed of doctors.' instead of 'She came from a family of doctors.' I was so naïve I didn't know that in the UK, using *breed* when describing someone is extremely derogatory. So perhaps you can imagine the expression on my colleague's face when one day, in a serious conversation about a particular lady, I casually said, 'She's a different kind of breed!'

What did you say?

I live in England and English people normally speak very softly. Unfortunately, I have difficulty hearing them. I found it terribly frustrating every time I was in a group and not able to follow the conversation. At some point, I actually thought I had become deaf. However, one afternoon while walking in the town centre, I heard someone behind me speak in my own language. I turned around and saw two Filipino women talking at normal volume. They were about three metres away from me yet I heard them. I was not deaf after all! I realised that my hearing difficulty was merely due to my brain not being switched on to English. It was a relief that my hearing was not that bad but sadly, this limitation negatively affected my chances of connecting with people whom I really wanted to connect with.

Was that funny?

British jokes can be very funny but most of the time they weren't to me. As most people know, every culture has its own style of humour.

Unfortunately, Philippine jokes are very different from UK jokes. Hence, I often looked silly when everyone was laughing and I was not. Not being able to share laughter with the people around me also reduced my chances of connecting with them on a more meaningful level.

Around the bush

I am a direct person, i.e., I say exactly what I mean most of the time. The British, on the other hand, have a tendency to beat around the bush. It's like being driven through little alleyways for thirty minutes to get to my destination when I could have been driven via the motorway in ten minutes. More often than not, the messages that I eventually received were so vague that the other person might as well have not said anything. What went wrong?

Imagine a group of immigrants trying to understand simple direct English. Many of them will cope. Next, imagine a group of immigrants trying to understand an English person who's beating around the bush. Many of them will not have a clue about what is being said. Understanding simple direct English requires only technical language skills while understanding English with subtleties requires a knowledge of the English culture.

I grew up in a very different environment with very different values, lifestyle and experiences from the British. Hence, I had very different perceptions from the Brits. For me and the other person to arrive at the same understanding, we must have some experiences in common so that I, as the listener, am able to interpret appropriately what the other person is trying to say.

Pitch it right

The British are perhaps the most polite people I've met in the manner in which they speak. In contrast, I being direct, was sometimes seen to be rude and insensitive. I can be knowingly both sometimes, but the difficulty happens when that's not the case. I felt misunderstood and over time, I developed the fear of being misinterpreted. Most of the time, I was wary of what I was about to say. To compensate for my directness, I tried to introduce some 'smoothers' into my manner of speaking. Sometimes it worked, sometimes it didn't. Where it did not work, I may have over-used my smoothers and would appear to be talking gibberish rather than assertively, as I had intended. I had difficulty getting the right pitch and I still have.

When I left Philippines, I did not really think that the language barrier would have a profound negative effect on me. I thought that if I could write and speak English, then surely I could live in the UK without a problem. I was so wrong! The above all caused my self-esteem to plummet.

Do what the Romans do

I should have known that taking this maxim to the extreme would not be good.

Although I left home when I was sixteen, I had never been outside of the Philippines prior to my move to the UK. Apart from my two weeks' Christmas holiday in the UK a few months before my permanent move, my exposure to life overseas was limited to TV shows, movies and printed media. I boarded my plane in May 1995 with only the slogan 'When in Rome, do as the Romans do' as my guide. Never in my life was I so unsure about what to do. After my first few months in the UK, I started observing seriously and copying other people. Most of the time it worked but at other times, it didn't.

In my humble opinion, Filipinos are generally more playful than the British. My family and close friends would know that quite often, I act like a girl. I believe I am reasonably mature in my outlook on life, but many of my ways are merely child-like. The Brits, on the other hand, would generally like to be seen as adults. To blend in, I copied others. Although at home I acted girly, outside my home, I was a grown-up woman behaving like a grown-up woman. Well, that was my intention anyway.

My attempt to behave like others gradually became problematic. I forced myself to become what I was not and what I didn't have the desire to become. In order to fit in, I masked myself and pretended to be someone else. Since I was only copying others and was not rooted in my own beliefs and principles, I would easily become confused when other people's behaviours manifested differently from the people

I was copying. I was like a log floating in the sea, being tossed by the tide as I kept on changing the people I copied something from.

After a while, I lost my own standards and with that loss, my ability to decide for myself diminished. I relied heavily on what my husband would say was acceptable or not, or fair or not, or good or bad, and so on. My thoughts were convoluted, my self-esteem spiralled down, and I no longer knew myself.

While writing this book, I tried to recall examples of when I copied other people. To my great surprise, I had difficulty remembering one. I know those tumultuous moments happened so why then can't I remember specific examples? Did I imagine those upsetting moments? Did my mind merely create them?

When I looked more closely at why, I came to the conclusion that there was no single event that was remarkable enough to be remembered. There were only little things that, again, while individually trivial, collectively made me unsure of myself. A trivial example is the known long-established debate as to whether one should spread the cream or the jam first over scones. It's a known debate even among Brits. When the Brits argue about this topic however, they're not looking to establish what's right or not. Their individual standards are already set and they have all the experiences of their native land to back their views. I, on the other hand, had little or no experience with scones and I was still forming my new standards in my new world. When presented with questions or situations that had no obvious right or wrong answers, I still had to form my reasons based on my limited experiences of my new land. When confronted with so many of those questions or situations at the same time, it got too much.

To buy myself time, I copied people. Sometimes I spread the jam first, sometimes it was the cream first, depending on whom I was with.

Colonial mentality + hierarchy culture

Of all the factors that affected me negatively, perhaps the mentality that anything from overseas was superior to anything in the Philippines was the one that I least suspected to be more significant than others.

During my childhood years in the Philippines, not many foreigners lived in our city and those who did were there most likely due to their jobs. They were quite influential as they were usually heads of companies or top managers. Filipinos looked up to them and called them *Sir* or *Ma'am*. To a young child, the scenario implied that all foreigners had higher ranks than Filipinos.

Also at that time, many Filipino products were indeed inferior to products from overseas. I remember that when I was seven or eight years old in grade school, sharpening my cheap native pencil was hard work. The lead easily broke and the wood around the lead was rough. My Dutch classmate's pencil, however, was very easy to sharpen as the lead was strong and the wood around the lead was smooth. Her sharp, robust, metal sharpener was also much better than my blunt, flimsy, plastic sharpener. At that young age and with such limited experience, it was so easy to believe that anything Filipino was inferior.

In addition to the colonial mentality, Philippines also has a hierarchical culture. It is very strong in both family and workplace contexts. There is a clear and unspoken understanding that a person with a higher rank must be treated with reverence by the people of lower ranks regardless of whether the former deserves that level of respect or not. Subordinates must address the person of higher rank as *Sir* or *Ma'am*, while subordinates are called merely by their first names. Challenging managers is not taken lightly and so Filipinos are all too used to saying 'Yes Sir' or 'Yes Ma'am' to their managers.

I did not have an inferiority complex problem when I was in the Philippines. Obviously, I had my own set of insecurities just like everyone has, but not to a scale of concern. Sadly, I observed an inferiority complex issue within me during my adjustment period in the UK. While working as an administrative assistant, I sometimes felt that one committee's treatment of me was meant for people lesser than themselves. For example, if there was an error on the file that they had given me to include in the agenda of a meeting, instead of checking first that they did not make the error themselves, they would immediately make comments that perhaps the file got distorted along the way before it was finally tabled. Those were indirect accusations against me and I did not defend myself because I did not have the courage to speak out. I was intimidated because they had higher ranks than me. I now know that not defending myself during those times was a mistake on my part and I attribute that largely to the concoction of colonial mentality and hierarchy culture in my subconscious mind. Over time, I developed the feeling of being a second-class citizen.

Tip: A friend once told me that projection is very important; sometimes more important than intelligence or ability. I wish I had clearly understood what she'd meant before my move.

A matter of perspective

Close-knit family values and the assistance that we had from family back in the Philippines were sorely missed when we started a family. I remember the day that my sister came back to our house from hospital when she'd had her first baby in the Philippines. I was there to receive the baby excitedly, and to offer the reassurance that we were there for her and she and her husband didn't have to worry about caring for the baby on their own.

In the UK, although my husband did his best to prepare the house for me and the baby, the overwhelming feeling of being on our own and of being unsure about what to do with our little addition was something I will never forget. Coming home with a newborn from the hospital to a dark house without food prepared on the table to help me recover from the physical, emotional and mental demands of delivery hit me hard.

Before my discharge from the hospital, my husband made a number of calls asking for instructions on how to cook *Tinolang Manok* (chicken soup). It is a food of choice after childbirth in the Philippines as it is seen as excellent for building energy and good for helping with breast milk production. I appreciate that he was doing everything he could, but those multiple calls were the last thing that I needed after more than forty-eight hours in the hospital without sleep.

It was evening when we returned home. As soon as I entered the house, strange feelings of uncertainty, fear and confusion swept over me. I didn't know where to start or what to do with the baby. I was torn between doing things for myself and tending to her needs. Suddenly, it dawned on me: it was no longer about just the husband and me – we now had a tiny baby who was completely relying on us.

My husband and I are both nurses. We were not new to looking after newborns or even unwell babies. But as professionals, we work in line with our nursing code of conduct, with policies and procedures to guide us in working alongside other medical and healthcare professionals to give the best possible care to our patients. At home, however, it was a completely different scenario with just the two us looking after someone very special.

To cut a long story short, I had a few more completely sleepless days and nights. On the seventh day, I had to seek help from my GP as I felt that another sleepless night would have driven me insane. I was prescribed anti-anxiety medication but because I was breastfeeding, I had anti-depressants instead, which was the safer option for a breastfeeding baby.

It was a really tough time for me which could have been different if I had been at home with the help of my family. Despite the UK government's programme to support parents through ante-natal and post-natal classes, and with all the other support for both mother and baby, I still felt helpless and traumatised by what I had been through.

Four years later, I had another baby. Armed with a different mindset learned in the previous years, I had a completely different experience. I was able to make full use of the help available from the government, family and friends. In this way, and in changing my lifestyle, I managed to raise two children without feeling the inadequacy that I had felt when I had our firstborn. I now truly believe that in life, a positive attitude will lead to positive outcomes.

Margie Deza Luistro
Philippines to United Kingdom

7: Dark moments

My life in the UK was not all doom and gloom. In fact, as of writing, I consider the UK as my home and there is nowhere on the planet at the moment that I would rather live than here. My transition period, however, was bleak. It was long, difficult and complex. A lot of things were grey, and no one understood me; not even my husband. I didn't even understand myself. I felt like I could not do anything right and the world was upside down.

Was it just me?

I had been living in the UK for twelve years when we took up residence in Australia for eight years. During my first decade in the UK, there were only a few Filipinos in our area. I would have liked to have developed friendships with them but unfortunately, their personalities were so different from mine.

My differences from the other Filipinos around that time weren't the same as my differences from British people. The former are not really the focus of this book but I thought I should explain a little bit about them as I believe they're relevant. I shared a similar background to the Filipinos I met in the UK – values/faith/psyche/education/etc – and so we shared many reference points. Although my points of view differed from theirs, we still all understood each other. I can't say the same for British people: there were few common reference points, and so there was little understanding between us.

Perhaps it would have been helpful if there had been at least one other Filipino who was on a similar wavelength to me at that time. We could have compared experiences. I suspect it would have been very helpful to me if I had found out then whether my feelings were normal for someone who had just moved to the country. Instead, I had so much doubt about whether something was wrong with me. I wondered whether I was going mad. I was scared.

Marriage

Every newly married couple goes through a stage of marital adjustment. Based on what I've read so far, the factors affecting adjustment include expectations, sleeping patterns, communication, ages, common decision-making, desires, family/friend relationships, leisure activities and standard of living, among others. Apart from those factors, my husband and I needed to adjust to each other's cultural backgrounds and we were so different.

They say that the first three years of marriage can be the most difficult. This timeframe perfectly coincided with the other adjustments I had to go through due to my move. Marital adjustment can be a real struggle on its own and combined with my other struggles, I faced a perfect storm.

My ability to cope with marital struggles was greatly affected by my struggles due to my move. Hence, the chances of my marriage surviving were reduced. There were pains both inside and outside of my home, so I had no respite. My husband was in pain too. He was in a difficult situation because he had to lift himself up when things were rough between us, and he had to lift me up too from my extra burdens.

Likewise, my ability to cope with my other struggles was greatly affected by my struggles within my marriage. There were times when I felt so hurt – indirectly – by my husband; I believe he felt the same about me too. The very person whom I expected to be with me in the abyss was my husband, yet he wasn't there. It was not because he didn't care – he cared very much. He just didn't understand me. We came from different environments, with different upbringings, with widely different sets of principles, different languages and so on. We didn't have many common reference points and building understanding between two people is so hard to achieve without them. He was there for me in spirit while I battled with my struggles due to my move. He was a very supportive husband. Sadly, however, at that time, it wasn't enough. I needed someone to understand me. Would it have been different if I had married a Filipino and we were living in the UK?

There is a famous phrase associated with relationships: 'the seven-year itch'. While writing this book, my husband and I have been married for twenty-seven years. It is due only to our strong love for each other that we are still together today. That is our most meaningful common reference point.

Masked façade

I've never been in so much mental stress and emotional pain than during those first five years in the UK. I was dealing with cultural, social, professional, marital and many other struggles at the same time. I cried so often at night and I had nightmares. Yet, I smiled a lot when I was with people. During the day, I was very friendly. Many of my work colleagues said that I always smiled even when the weather was miserable, dark, and wet. Little did they know that my true feelings were not so different from the weather.

Why did I keep on smiling? Was it because it was a habit? Well, I naturally smile a lot but before, they were genuine smiles. Why did I keep on smiling? Maybe because in Caucasian movies, characters make efforts to appear strong in spite of all their miseries. I did what the Romans do. Why did I keep on smiling? Perhaps I didn't want to feel embarrassed about how weak I was at that time. Perhaps I did not want to admit that maybe my decision to move to the UK was wrong. Perhaps I didn't want my husband to be the subject of gossips. Perhaps I was trying to lift myself up. Perhaps I was desperate to blend in and looking miserable wouldn't help. Why did I keep on smiling? Perhaps it was a combination of all of the above. Perhaps none of the above. Perhaps all of the above.

The point is, I was unsure why I kept on smiling. However, smiling or not, I was not my natural self. I wore a mask. I wanted to blend in so I tried to look self-controlled like a stereotypical Brit. I bottled up everything so that at nights, I screamed from nightmares and my pillow was usually damp.

8: What I did

I survived my adjustment period in the UK. It probably took me about five years to feel that though life was difficult, it was not the end of the world; three more years to feel life was difficult but that things were getting better; and two more years to feel that life was, indeed, better. After my twelfth year, we moved to Australia. We went back after eight years and by then, I was well adjusted to my life as an explorer and had learned to embrace things, good or bad, as they came along.

Perhaps by now you are wondering what I did to survive: quite a few things, actually. There wasn't one single solution but a combination of a few.

Nothing

I did nothing. Luckily, time does wonders and a number of my struggles disappeared over a period of time without me even noticing it.

I hadn't appreciated heritage buildings before. I grew up with modern structures so to my eyes, a majority of old buildings looked grubby. I also used to get really irritated if old buildings didn't function as efficiently as they should. For example, I was annoyed that the gradient of rake at Brighton's Theatre Royal was so steep that the view of someone sitting at the back of a level was partly obstructed by the front of the next level up. I'd wished then that the theatre would be demolished and replaced by a properly working modern theatre.

Over time, without making any effort at all, my preference for buildings changed. I now would like old buildings with architectural or historical significance to be preserved. I now greatly appreciate the beauty of old architecture and I've become tolerant of their shortcomings due to their age. I don't know when exactly the change in me happened, but it did.

Another example is the food. In the previous chapter, I mentioned that the dishes in the UK were bland and I cringed whenever I ate them. Well, I now enjoy food with no or very little seasoning. Over time, my taste buds changed. I didn't plan or do anything to cause the change;

my taste buds simply adapted. Having said that, one must never underestimate the effects of food in one's life. This is something often overlooked by immigrants but one that would most likely cause some difficulty; the duration of which will vary from one person to another.

It dawned on me while writing this book that my taste has changed without me doing anything. Could it be that adjustments relating to sense organs need only time? Over the years, I've grown accustomed to the UK's cold weather too, and I cannot recall doing anything specific to adapt.

Familiarise, familiarise, familiarise

There is an old saying that goes 'Familiarity breeds contempt.' However, there is also a relatively new saying that goes 'Familiarity breeds content.' As for me, I did find comfort after my initiation into some of the British habits that I had considered to be weird, strange or peculiar.

It didn't take long before I completely got used to tearing off the gift-wrapping whenever I received presents, stopped staring at pink hair, and understood that Brits don't say 'no'. You have to note that when you suggest something and the other person says 'That's interesting.', what they're really saying is 'I am not interested.' Worse, if that person says 'That's a bold proposal.', that sometimes means 'You fu**ing id**t!'

However, there are some things that, although I have become familiar with them, I still cannot relate to. For example, I learned to say thank you when someone says I am an attractive lady though deep in my heart, I really don't understand that.

Sometimes, I had to put myself into the shoes of Brits in order to really understand why they do what they do. In some cases, I created a laboratory environment where I could actually do what the Brits do. For example, I was quite conservative in my fashion choices relative to Brit ladies my age. So, when we went to Miami where no one knew us, I wore a bikini that I had made myself so I could bare myself as much as possible. My top was made of two 4x4cm (roughly) heart-shaped pieces of fabric attached to a string fabric, while my bottom was a 6x8cm (roughly) heart-shaped piece of fabric also attached to a string fabric. Even on Miami Beach where bikinis were a common sight, my yellow heart bikini attracted attention (and I have a few photos to prove it!).

The experience gave me a taste of how Brit ladies on Brighton beach might feel when they wear skimpy bikinis or go topless. I knew then I definitely wouldn't make a habit of wearing such a bikini, but I now have something of an understanding of why ladies do it, or how they feel when they do it. And in case you're wondering, yes, I did go topless in France to find out how that feels too!

Change habits

Habits can be hard to get rid of but, over time, they are one of the easiest things to change. Yes, it took some effort to remember and restrain myself from extending my arms downward in front of me while passing in between two people in a conversation, or to remember to hold the door for the person behind me. Nevertheless, my muscle memory took over reasonably quickly. I don't even remember when my old habits left me, and the new ones took over.

There were also some habits that took a while before I was able to change them. For example, mall weekend trips used to be my most common leisure activity. When I moved to UK, it took me a while to get used to the idea that, at that time, not many stores were open on weekends. Unlike the other examples, this has nothing to do with muscle memory. Rather, it's a type of habit that was more about mindset. At some point, I realised that I simply needed to engage in other types of activities instead of going to malls. So I attended dance classes, enrolled in short courses, or went for walks in the countryside. In addition, there were always household chores that needed doing over the weekends. In the span of a year, possibly two, I forgot all about weekend mall trips.

Accept the consequences and rewards

There were things that were difficult to change but that were simply not core to my principles or values. So, when I got used to more trivial things, I regained some headspace and was able to work around those non-core issues.

To solve my problem with clothes, whenever I visited Philippines, I bought clothing of my size in bulk which would last me for five years. In exchange for this hassle, I often received compliments in the UK about my fashion sense. People noticed that my outfits were unusual and different from the typical British style and that they looked nice.

I cannot cook and I am lazy at cooking, so I've been largely dependent on Chinese/Japanese/Thai restaurants in the UK to alleviate my craving for Filipino dishes. Once in a while, I get invited to Filipino gatherings and they help ease my cravings. I haven't really found yet a good workaround regarding this issue. However, over time, I've learned to accept this gap in my life in exchange for other non-food things I have gained while living in the UK.

Perhaps the hardest challenge I had in this category was the lack of meaningful friendships in the UK in the early years. Winning meaningful friendships in one's native country is not an easy task anyway so gaining meaningful friendships in another country is, understandably, even harder. Patience and mixing with British people were the key approaches for me in tackling this issue. I lived in loneliness in the early years but I also lived in hope that in the near future, my relations with people in the UK would bear fruit. They did, and I cannot see any reason why it wouldn't be the same for other immigrants in this country.

In short, I accepted the gaps in my life due to leaving Philippines, and I embraced the rewards I received due to living in the UK. Once I had done that, my life in my new country became so much easier. Of course, it's more easily said than done but over time, it gets easier. Mindset is key.

Avoid avoiding practicalities

According to a Russian proverb, 'Where necessity speaks it demands.' The challenges I had of this type varied a lot from trivial to critical, and they all gave me no choice but to face them head-on.

At the more trivial end of the spectrum, I mentioned in the earlier part of this book that every year, I slip when the roads get icy after snowfall. I researched and found out that I needed to learn to walk on ice. I walked very slowly, and chose carefully the areas where I walked; preferably, where there was a rail (or an equivalent) that I could grab just in case. I started using backpacks so that my arms were free for balance. Later, I learned that I should point my toes outward a bit and to walk flat-footed to keep my centre of gravity over my feet. While I walked everywhere looking like a penguin, many of the Brits walked gracefully like figure skaters.

One of the more critical challenges that I couldn't escape was the need to re-learn English. There is a noticeable difference between American English (which I learned while growing up in the Philippines) and British English. Luckily, I had enormous help with my grammar from my husband. Poor bloke; in addition to his own work, he also had to review my work deliverables. He still does!

Apart from grammar, I also needed to deal with the subtleties of the language. Since a big influence on the subtleties of a language is cultural, there were few shortcuts for me in learning them. I continued mixing with native English speakers because it's only through living and engaging with a culture that a language can be fully understood. Certainly (but perhaps to a lesser degree), familiarity with slang and terminologies also depends on familiarity with the culture. My exposure and submersion over time were key to my progress in overcoming such language difficulties.

I wouldn't say now that it is bad that the Brits beat around the bush so much. I am better now in understanding them than before because, again, I took steps to extend my network to include non-Filipinos. By doing that, I increased my exposure to the complexities of the English language. Where I really cannot understand, I now have the confidence to ask and, if appropriate, explain why I asked. Based on my experience, native English speakers understand the challenge I have and are happy to say what they've said in a more understandable manner.

In dealing with negotiations or arguments, I found that I'm better at expressing myself through writing than through speaking. Hence, whenever possible, and to buy myself some time to improve my speaking skills, I communicate via email especially where it matters that I express my views clearly. I hand-delivered a few letters to my husband. Also, in communications where sensitivity is required, I try to stick to facts (with no or few subtleties which I may use wrongly) and, whenever possible, I ask my husband to check my email or letter to see whether the tone is as I intended it to be. Over time, I got better but I still have some way to go.

In a more formal, corporate setup, my comprehension has improved over time which is due, I believe, to exposure and submersion. However, at times when I suspect that my understanding may have been incorrect, say, while facilitating a workshop, I paraphrase what has been said and ask for verification. I was only able to do that though when I had regained my confidence. Also, I no longer hesitate to ask at least one colleague (usually one of the project team members) to verify that the transcript I've written is aligned with their understanding before I circulate it to our clients.

What is really fascinating is the realisation that I now think in English. I didn't notice when the switch happened but I'm glad it did as it made my life easier. To this day, however, I still have some difficulty with English and I've accepted that my brain is simply not wired for it. Since language is such a fundamental ingredient in one's survival outside one's native country, I persevere in learning it by appreciating my husband's corrections to my writing and speech, and by constantly being with English native speakers. It is not just a choice, but a necessity.

Sadly, some immigrants who have difficulty grasping the English language tend to surround themselves only with other immigrants from their native country. That is not a bad thing but it is limiting one's development in communication skills. Chances are, they will never embrace the culture of their new country and, as a result, won't be able to integrate effectively with the British people. It is likely that they will forever feel like second-class citizens in the UK.

Express myself

As more of my challenges were removed over time, I started becoming sure of myself again. The more I understood the British culture and the more I was able to anticipate how society would react to my thoughts/speech/actions, the more stable I became. My language skills improved too and I felt less afraid that I might be saying something that was different from what I meant to say. All the above contributed to me regaining my confidence and feeling more connected with this once totally foreign country.

Having gained confidence, I now express myself when I feel it is appropriate or necessary. For example, I now feel comfortable telling people that I prefer meeting indoors because the direct sun makes me ill. I can now joke about trying to catch up with a group when everyone else, except me, goes walking at a hundred miles an hour. I now hesitate less in requesting people not to lick their fingers in turning over pages if they will be giving the sheets to me afterwards.

Reactions to my self-expressions varied. Oftentimes, it resulted in something good. Sometimes, it created undesirable results. However, the unpredictability of these reactions no longer bother me much because I have now gained enough knowledge and formed my own standards (to a good extent) of what I think is appropriate, and what is not, in the UK.

I am who I am

I mentioned earlier in this book that, at some point, I no longer knew myself. I let the saying 'Do what the Romans do' guide me and that ripped my confidence from me. When I realised what was happening, I stepped back a little, looked at myself and thought hard about what could be done. Yes, for some things that don't really matter, I can keep on doing what the Romans do. So, if the Brits want to spread cream first before jam on their scones, then I'll follow that. However, I cannot simply abandon my principles because everyone else's are different from mine. Either I face the price of living according to my principles in a country where they are not welcome, or I pack and leave the UK. I have decided to stay for now. So, though the Brits are happy to bow down before their Royal Family/Clan, I will definitely not follow that custom and I am prepared to lose connections with people who cannot accept my view on that.

While in the process of looking at myself, I came to realise that many of my principles have changed. I have become a very different person from the Ging that left Philippines in 1995. Living in the UK has made me realise that, actually, being a multi-cultural person is very enriching and I must keep on changing. This time, I must not simply copy, but adopt different principles when my conscience tells me to.

Living my life according to what my conscience told me once more was a newfound freedom. I regained my confidence, I became less dependent on my husband, and it enabled me to interact with Brits on an equal footing. I did not see myself a second-class citizen anymore, so gone was any unjustified colonial mentality in me. Shortly after this change, I sensed that people started treating me as their equal. That certainly contributed to my feeling of belonging in the UK.

At work, I binned the excessive hierarchical culture innate in me. I finally believed that my managers simply play their roles in a project team (just like I play my role in a team) and I am as important as they are. As people, they are no more and no less than me. I treat them with respect and I expect equal respect from them; anything less is not acceptable.

Reconfirming who I am was definitely a very significant factor in my feeling happier in the UK. I learned that people's treatment of me depended heavily on how I projected myself. If someone feels that he or she is a second-class citizen, then chances are, that person will be treated as such. I would like to emphasise just how important it was that I finally re-learnt merely to be myself. I hope that you will contemplate on this during your own journey.

Tip: People respond according to how you project yourself. If you want to be treated like a first-class citizen, then act like one.

Marriage

The things I did to adjust in the UK were done in a somewhat progressive manner. Those changes that did not require any direct actions from me generally happened first. They led to some of my headspace being freed which enabled me to address the next set of adjustments, and so on and so forth.

I am unsure which type of adjustment category my marriage fell into. Cultural differences between spouses must never be underestimated. As mentioned previously, my husband and I have made enormous adjustments for each other over these past years. What I did, what he did, or what we did is, mostly likely, not worth mentioning because each couple's circumstances are different. However, what I can offer is the knowledge that it was only because of our deep love for each other that my husband and I are still together today in spite of our cultural differences. Apart from that, all other books about marriage counselling are likely to be better references than my narrative.

Tip: Make sure you marry someone who truly loves you and whom you truly love.

Interlude 2

Since I left Philippines for good in 1995, I have had five trips back to my home country. The first one was in 1997, then 2002, followed by another in 2004, again in 2008, and lastly in 2013/2014. It's fascinating and strange remembering those trips. It was fascinating because I can see the change in my attitude towards my native culture with each trip. It's strange because never did I ever imagine myself relating to British culture more than the Philippine culture.

Two years after leaving Philippines, I returned with so much excitement to my island country. I reconnected with family and friends as if those two years had never happened. I ate my favourite dishes like a pig, and I visited the memory lane of my childhood with glee. I was home again.

My second trip, seven years after I left Philippines, was not as exciting as the first. I was ecstatic to see my immediate family and close friends, but I started to feel uncomfortable with a few things that I used to be comfortable with. My discomfort was more pronounced during my third trip, nine years after leaving Philippines. If not for my immediate family, most likely, I would not have taken that trip. By then, most of my close friends had already left the country anyway.

Thirteen years after I left Philippines, I did not have the desire to go back for any reason except to see my immediate family. Nineteen years after I left Philippines, I couldn't wait to leave at the end of my six-month stay there.

I have become a foreigner in my native country. I now see funny/weird/strange things that did not seem that way to me before. I am now sensitive to things that didn't really catch my attention before. I now hate things that I only disliked before. Many of the things that I hate are not unique to Philippines but their magnitude stands out there, compared with the other countries I've lived in.

9: The same, no more

Sometimes, one needs to leave a place and come back before one notices things that have always been there but which were never seen.

When I left Philippines, I started to see a different set of truths. I saw another world in the UK in both physical and ideological terms. When I went back to the Philippines, I realised that there were many things that had always been there that I had never noticed before. They were part of my daily life which my brain had become accustomed to and stopped noticing. Living outside of the Philippines for a period of time resulted in my brain getting used to other things. So when I came back to my home country, I started noticing things that I had missed before. I have included a few below.

Hold (not!) the bloody door

In the UK, when people go through doors, they hold the doors open for the next person as a courtesy (see Chapter 4). In a span of two years, I acquired that habit so on my first trip back to the Philippines, when I went through a door, I held it open for the next person. Whenever I did so, Filipinos looked at me with a confused expression. Only then did I remember that I should have merely let go of the door after I'd been through.

I found myself in a similar situation previously when I entered a lift with my hand stretched slightly forward between two Caucasian males in the UK (see Chapter 4). The difference this time was, although I found my experiences in the Philippines funny, I did not feel embarrassed at all. I knew exactly what was happening and I knew the Filipino culture well enough to be able to guess what Filipinos in those situations were thinking. With that knowledge, I was in control of how to respond to those awkward situations.

Beauty queens and kings

Beauty contests are extremely important in the Philippines, e.g., the Miss Universe pageant is like an annual national event. There appears to be always an excuse to have a beauty contest, e.g., at university or school events, city or town religious festivals, company celebrations, sports leagues, professional assembly, alumni homecoming events, product marketing, etc. This is more so with female than with male pageants.

I used to watch a couple of beauty contests on an annual basis. Since I left Philippines twenty-seven years ago, I haven't watched any. It wasn't a conscious decision on my part but a natural process within myself as I grew older. Influenced by UK's cold and resistant attitude towards beauty contests, there are many other things that I would rather spend my time on than pageants.

I do appreciate physical beauty but to me, it needs to be in a context more meaningful than women parading in swimsuits and stating 'world peace' as their wish during interviews. I can see that these contests can be fun and entertaining when taken lightly, and I would watch them again while killing time or engaging in frivolous bonding times with friends. However, I cringe at the fact that beauty pageants are taken seriously by many. In a nation that treats beautiful people as superior to others merely because of their appearances, Philippines is certainly not the place for an ordinary face like mine.

Excuse my new manners

I was having a casual dinner with a very dear friend in a relaxed restaurant in Manila. Knowing that I'd just washed my hands, I did not hesitate to lick my two fingers to remove a few droplets of sauce. When I looked at my friend, I saw that familiar expression on his face! I had forgotten that licking fingers in public in the Philippines is considered gross. He looked so shocked. He didn't say anything and we didn't talk about it, but I knew what those eyes were saying and what the brief silence between us meant. I won't forget that look and I thought it was funny!

How could I have forgotten?

On my second trip back to Philippines, I noticed that I was starting to forget some Filipino vocabulary. In the UK, I rarely speak Pilipino because my social and work networks are mostly people from other cultures. My husband is English, for a start. The most frequent opportunities I get to speak Pilipino are when I call my family.

I am actually fascinated when I'm reminded that sometimes I forget the language I grew up with and used every day until I was twenty-four years old. In more recent years, I have also noticed that I am having a little difficulty constructing Pilipino sentences. I am unsure whether this is due to my long absence from the Philippines or worse, due to my age. It could be both.

100 miles per hour

'Slow down Ging!' That's what my family and friends in the Philippines have said to me a number of times. During my transition period in the UK, I struggled keeping up with the pace when walking with others. I didn't realise that over the years, I've become better in adopting the normal UK walking speed. So I was very surprised when family and friends in the Philippines asked me to slow down. I was on a race while all others were strolling on a beach. In the UK, I was the one strolling on a beach. Funny!

We're a family

Philippine society is very family-oriented. I grew up in a culture where people stay in their extended family members' houses whenever they visit. I suspect this was initially the norm but over time, it became the practice to save money. Unless the reason is economics, which I fully understand, I now find this practice weird. I can no longer relate to people choosing to stay in one house where there's not enough beds for the sake of being together for twenty-four hours (even when they're sleeping for about a third of that period). I would rather stay somewhere else more comfortable while sleeping so that I can rest and enjoy more my time together with family and friends the next day.

When my husband and I went back to the Philippines for the first time, we stayed in a hotel rather than in my parents' house. I needed to explain to my immediate family prior to our trip that we will not be staying in my parents' house because we wanted our own space. In the UK, that is usual and something that doesn't warrant any explanation. My immediate family fully understood but it raised a few eyebrows among others. I didn't explain because I didn't have to and I didn't want to.

The raised eyebrows would have caused me to worry if this scenario had happened during my transition period in the UK. In contrast, I didn't worry when I experienced it in the Philippines. I believe, again, that the reason is that, I knew how Filipino society thought and behaved, and so I knew how to react in such situations. I knew what was at stake and my reaction was based on what I already knew. It was so different during my adjustment period in the UK. I was close to being clueless as to how the British would think and behave, and therefore, I was clueless as to how to react and how to assess the effects of any unpleasantries.

Kili-kili power

The weather in the Philippines can be oppressive. The combination of high temperatures and high humidity can bring out many kinds of smell, including body odours. Body odour is commonly known as '*kili-kili* power' in the country; *kili-kili* means armpit in Pilipino.

Fortunately, Filipinos generally have high standards in personal hygiene so it is not normally a problem being in a small crowd, e.g., public transportation, offices, etc. There may be instances when you come across people who smell. Usually, they are those who also behave strangely, or those who do demanding manual labour. With Philippine heat, I can totally understand that the situation can be inevitable for those that do manual labour.

Every time I went back to the Philippines, I was reminded that personal hygiene is one of the Filipino traits that I wish I could see more of in the UK. It would be refreshing, literally!

Too hot

On my second trip, I started to struggle with Philippine climate. On my third trip, I definitely struggled. After I'd acclimatised to the UK's generally cool climate, I found Philippine climate unbearably hot even during the cooler months.

To me, one of the most uncomfortable things to do in hot places is to wear a bra. In the UK, there were many times when I didn't wear a bra in the summer. Yes, some people stared but letting the contour of my nipples protrude through my clothing was not a stigma, as it is in the Philippines.

I can no longer imagine how I survived in my younger years when I had to wear a bra every time I was out of our house. Maybe I was younger then and more tolerant to irritants but these days, wearing a bra in my native country is punishing to me. The discomfort stops being trivial when I feel sweltering hot and am suffering from headaches. Luckily, when visiting Philippines, I usually travelled in a taxi or a private car, which was a relief because it gave me the chance to unhook my bra while in the vehicle. A temporary respite!

10: No thanks

Sometimes, one needs to leave a place before one realises that there were things in the past that may have appeared insignificant but are now significant, and vice versa. These realisations have had a significant impact on me and have caused me to reassess the things that are important to me. They also caused me to start re-evaluating which country is truly my home. I describe a few in this chapter.

Food

I enjoy eating and, if prepared and presented in a hygienic manner, my favourite cuisine is generally still Filipino. Unfortunately, my exposure to other food cultures has somewhat affected my enjoyment of Filipino dishes.

After a few years of living in the UK, I realised that it was not that the English food was tasteless. It was rather my over-exposure to salt and sugar when growing up in the Philippines that has influenced my early dislike of food in the UK. As years passed, my tolerance to salt and sugar diminished and I became sensitive to salty and sweet tastes. The favourable by-product of that was, I started sensing the natural taste of fish, the healthy fresh taste of vegetables, and the true taste of lean beef. Whenever I visited Philippines, my taste buds normally needed to acclimatise for a few weeks before I could eat most dishes without overly tasting the salt, sugar or monosodium glutamate added.

One thing I also learned as soon as I arrived in the UK was to eat my food while it's hot. Keeping food at room temperature encourages bacterial growth and when the amount of bacteria has reached a particular level, one could suffer from food poisoning. Many Filipinos, including my immediate family, have the habit of preparing meals without considering the exact eating time. For example, lunch might be cooked and placed on the table at 11:30a.m. ready for consumption at around midday. Although my tummy was used to that practice before, I now hesitate to consume food under those circumstances, especially meat or seafood dishes. My first, and so far only food poisoning experience, was quite enough.

You can take the girl out of the Philippines but you cannot take the Philippines out of the girl. That's me with some of the processed food I love from the Philippines. I love tocino, chorizo, tapa, and the like. These are all processed meats that require chemicals during preparation. I remember my mother making some homemade ones and she had to soak the meat with different kinds of liquid poured from pharmacy-like bottles. To this day, I still enjoy eating those processed meats but unlike before, I now eat them in moderation.

Idiotic rules

Philippines is a conservative country but not to the extreme. When you look at how people dress up, you'll find many women wearing shorts, sleeveless tops, off-the-shoulder necklines, backless tops, etc; and many men wearing an earring, long hair, etc. That's not a criticism but rather a positive comment about having the liberty to choose what to wear within reason.

Sadly, I couldn't say the same thing when I went to get a National Bureau of Investigation (NBI) clearance. NBI is the equivalent to the USA's FBI. During that time, an in-person application was required so that a photo of the applicant could be taken at an NBI office and processed completely in-house. Fair enough, I can see the logic in that.

When I arrived, I immediately saw a sign stuck on the wall saying that NBI will not process one's clearance if one was wearing a sleeveless top. A reason was not given only that they did not allow sleeveless attire in photos. I checked but there was nothing stated anywhere in any printed literature to confirm that that was the case. Luckily, I was wearing a top with sleeves at that time. Otherwise, I would have been very cross for two reasons. First, I would have wasted my time having travelled for two hours in hot weather for nothing. Second, I didn't see any logic in the policy. Sleeveless tops were common tops in the country and were being worn by women at that time, even in a professional context.

After a few days and still feeling quite irritated with the policy, I asked friends why it was necessary to wear sleeved tops for NBI photos. One of the reasons given was that one's appearance on legal documents must be formal. I didn't buy that. A person can be wearing a sleeveless top and still look formal. Another reason given was that one must look one's best on an NBI photo to show respect to officers. I didn't buy that either. The purpose of photos for an NBI clearance is to establish the identity of the bearer and definitely not to please officers. Wearing sleeveless tops could actually help when checking identities because sleeveless tops may reveal some body marks, e.g., tattoos/scars/warts/etc, which otherwise would not be visible.

Until now, I still haven't received a convincing reason for the policy. I don't know whether the rationale is related to religion or not. If it is, at least I am able to understand why the policy is so conservative. Without a clear and convincing reason however, I regard that policy as idiotic and backward.

Obviously, idiotic rules are not unique to the Philippines. I'm sure that there are idiotic rules in the UK too that are only noticed by Brits after they've been away from the UK. I wonder whether I would have questioned such a policy if I hadn't lived outside of the Philippines. The fact that rules are not always right and might be outdated makes me appreciate more the things that I've seen outside of the Philippines.

Filipino time

Shamefully, 'Filipino time' refers to the notorious habit of Filipinos being late – sometimes several hours late. Even events will have lateness built in. For example, if a concert is advertised to start at say 7:00p.m., that really means it will start at 8:00p.m.

I did not like this trait before and I now hate it. In all of my trips back to the Philippines, I experienced 'Filipino time' moments and they drove me nuts. I am a busy person and I often struggle to find time for myself. To waste my time merely waiting for someone whose only excuse is 'I overslept' or 'I haven't noticed the time' is not acceptable. Worse, the lateness is sometimes the medium to demonstrate one's inflated ego or to exert one's superiority over others by making them wait. Someone who is constantly late without valid reason has no respect for other people's time. Hence, that person does not deserve others' respect either.

I noticed that my patience towards this behaviour diminished further on successive trips. Although I already didn't like it before I left

Philippines, I put up with it because it was the only 'normal' I knew then. I have changed and I'm sure I'd be irritable most of the time if I had to deal with this way of life again.

Ships from my window

It was five minutes before touchdown. When I looked out of the plane window, I saw smog over Manila! The first thing that had saddened me during my previous three visits to the Philippines had been the seriousness of the pollution, especially in Metro Manila, which includes the capital city of Manila and its surrounding areas.

I spent six months in Metro Manila in 2013/2014 and I coughed for about five of them. It got so bad at some point that I had to see a doctor three times within three weeks just to make sure that I was not suffering from something serious. There was nothing permanently wrong with my respiratory system but I needed to take some antibiotics for an extended period to address my infection.

During those six months, I lived on the seventeenth floor of one of the posh buildings in Metro Manila's financial district. From my apartment, I could see many other high-rise buildings that, on a bad day, looked as if their tops were ascending into an opaque sky. Two weeks before I was scheduled to go home, I was looking out of the window and was in deep thought about what I needed to prepare for my departure. Suddenly, I noticed something in the distance that appeared like a submarine. I blinked a few times to clear my vision and voila, I couldn't believe what I saw. I saw a ship! After five-and-a-half months of living in that apartment, I knew only then that I had sea views from my wall-to-wall and floor-to-ceiling glass wall. After about ten minutes, I saw many other ships. I almost fell off my chair in disbelief! That was a clear day and the only day out of six months when I enjoyed what I had actually paid for for a high-rise, high-end apartment with sea views.

Pollution is a common concern around the world and the UK has its own share of this serious problem too. However, when compared to the pollution problem in the Philippines, the UK's air quality feels quite tame and relatively safe. The pollution level in the Philippines is quite amplified compared to those in other countries I have lived in.

Spaghetti traffic

While in the Philippines in 2013/2014, I stayed initially in Manila (capital city) and travelled every day to my workplace in Makati (financial district). On a good day, and if travelling by taxi, it would only take roughly thirty minutes to arrive at my destination. However, due to heavy traffic almost always, my everyday one-way travel could last up to two hours.

Traffic problems in the Philippines are mostly self-inflicted. Basically, drivers do not follow rules and so, the flow of the traffic often results in a spaghetti-like chaos where stranded vehicles face in different directions.

After one week of sitting in a giant "car park" for two hours each way every day, and breathing in all the fumes, I decided to move to somewhere that was within walking distance from work.

I was used to that kind of traffic in Manila in my younger years. Nowadays, I no longer wish to live in a place where such hold-ups are likely to be an everyday part of my life. Of all the cities I've lived in, the traffic conditions in Metro Manila top my chart as the most unbearable. The worst part is knowing that the hassles are self-inflicted. If only there were discipline, things would not reach that level of mess.

Measure of success

In many societies, including British society, success is most commonly measured by wealth and rank, and of all the countries I have lived in, this is especially true of the Philippines.

For me however, success is about achieving one's goals in life. It's a simple formula: success = goals achieved. For example, if someone wants to be a playworker (one of the lowest paid jobs in the UK in 2021), then as long as that person is happy in that role and is not dependent on others, that is success. If that person is not able to go to the cinema, or is not able to go on holiday due to a limited budget, then it doesn't really matter because going to cinemas or on holidays are not that person's goals.

Living outside of the Philippines for twenty-seven years means that I have very little knowledge about present-day life in my native country. Luckily, my six-month trip in 2013/2014 gave me the chance to catch up with news about my distant family and my friends. On that trip down memory lane, I often heard comments along the lines of 'David (not real name), your ex-colleague, is now very successful. He owns a big house, drives a nice car, and travels abroad frequently.' From my perspective, if those things are really what David wants, then yes, he is successful and good on him.

I do not criticise people who want financial abundance, nor do I criticise people who want something else instead. One of our cleaners in the UK did not want to be doing anything else and, sometimes, I envied her. What disturbs me though is the very common and hasty conclusion that if someone has obtained wealth or has climbed the corporate ladder, then they're definitely successful; while others who live humbly are considered by society as either less successful or failures. Sadly, in my experience, this belief is amplified in the Philippines more than anywhere else I've lived.

I am grateful to the UK for revealing to me that there is more to success than merely gaining financial possessions or climbing the ranks. In my eyes, one can be a cleaner and a complete success, while another can be a CEO and a complete failure. I am convinced that I can no longer live in a society where monetary wealth and rank are strongly considered to be the only yardsticks of success. I believe I would feel choked.

11: Not for me anymore

Sometimes, one needs to leave a place before one realises how badly one hates some aspects of one's native culture. In my case, having been back five times to the Philippines, I have confirmed to myself that it's time to say goodbye to them.

Many of the people I know who moved to live outside of the Philippines chose to move back or are choosing to move back in the future for their retirement. They look forward to having a relaxing life with helpers to do the housework and to the fact that their overseas pension will go a long way due to favourable exchange rates.

Whenever I have asked myself the same question over the past twenty years, my answer has always been 'possibly' or 'definitely not'. For the past ten years, it's been the latter response. I analysed myself to clearly understand the reason(s) why my final answer is different from those of people I know. Yes, I desire a relaxing and abundant life. However, there are things that I just cannot live with, a few of which I list below.

I know no one

Of all the countries I've lived in, there is nowhere else where the concept of 'who-you-know' is more important than in the Philippines. This culture is so ingrained in Philippine society it exists everywhere at all levels. My earliest recollection of this practice was at a kid's beauty contest. (No, I didn't join the contest.) Over a lunch break, I overheard a judge hinting which contestant she was going to let to win because the contestant's parents were her peers. I was only a kid, not even ten years old, but that memory stuck into my mind because it was my first time to feel angry about the blatant unfairness in the society in which I was growing up. That emotion, at such a young age, was so strong that I grew up vouching to avoid that way of life as much as I could. Until now, I've never mentioned to anyone what I'd heard over that lunch break. The contestant that was crowned was a friend, a very nice girl, and it was not her fault that she 'won'.

I came from a family with a humble background. Just like any good parents, my parents worked hard to give myself and my siblings the best chances in life. They were not influential nor well-connected so the fruits of their labours were mainly achieved through their own efforts. While growing up, I lost out on opportunities to many others due to the fact that my family did not have connections. That led to me hating such a practice and to striving to get to where I am now through my own merits.

The injustice of the 'who you know' culture is widely accepted in Philippine society. Filipinos generally acknowledge that it is wrong, yet, it is a normal way of life. To give readers an idea what it was like to live in that culture, imagine the following scenarios:

At a doctor's clinic, appointments are on a first-come-first-served basis. You are given your number when you arrive at the clinic. After waiting for more than three hours for your turn, someone who has just arrived is seen by the doctor before you.

In the days when phone lines were scarce, you would submit your application for a phone line and five years later you would still be waiting for a phone. Meanwhile, someone who had rich connections might apply and get their phone installed the following week.

You apply for a job and although you know you are far better than the other applicant, you don't get the job because the other applicant had influence. It was quite common for job applicants to think about who they might know in a company before thinking whether they're qualified for the job.

A loved one is dying. You are told that there is no bed available in the hospital. However, you later find out that a patient was admitted about the same time that you enquired, just because the other patient knew a senior manager in the hospital.

I have never accepted the above scenarios and I just know that I could never accept them as the norms of a place where I would choose to live permanently. Having said that, I am not without sin in taking advantage of the 'who you know' culture when things get desperate. Shamefully, I still make use of connections when things get desperate regarding whatever remaining affairs I still have to deal with in my native country. I was not comfortable about it, every time though. It is extremely difficult to do things cleanly when the environment dictates otherwise.

Discipline, where art thou?

My husband and I explored Malls of Asia (MoA), a shopping mall so big it could easily engulf an English village (or more). After lots of walking and not carrying even a single shopping bag, we decided it was time to go back to our hotel. It was about thirty minutes before the mall closing time in the evening.

We went to the taxi rank and, based on my vague recollection, we were probably the fourth or fifth in the line. Unfortunately, taxis were so rare and a taxi phone order service was not available then. Before we made it to the front, the malls had closed and many people had joined the taxi rank queue. It didn't take long before the queue had extended to about twenty metres in length.

Since it was taking very long for taxis to arrive, many people started losing their patience. To my disgust, those at the end of the queue started to hail taxis arriving at the rank. Also to my disgust, the drivers accommodated those people at the back instead of driving past to offer their service to those at the front of the queue. Not surprisingly, there was friction between the people in front and the people at the back of the queue.

Having waited for so long, I too, lost my patience. I saw two policemen half a block away who were oblivious to what was happening. I left my husband in the queue and walked towards them. I described what was happening and asked them politely to help bring order back to the queue. Sadly, they ignored me saying that it was not really their job to do that. It may have been true that police officers are not responsible for managing taxi rank queues. However, friction was brewing among the people in the queue so I believe it was not unreasonable to ask police officers to intervene at that point. After a short heated argument, I asked for their names so that I could report them to their superiors the following day. Only then did they reluctantly agree to help and to walk with me to the taxi rank.

Looking back, I am grateful that the two policemen eventually agreed to help me instead of putting a bullet in my head for telling them to do their job (policemen carry guns in the Philippines).

Discipline is so scarce in the Philippines, and I have hated that ever since I was old enough to understand. No country is exempt from that problem. However, the lack of discipline in the Philippines is beyond comparison when it comes to what I've seen in other countries I've lived in. I truly believe that many of the everyday difficulties being faced by Filipinos are being caused by our own lack of discipline. While growing up in the Philippines, I viewed such behaviour with contempt but I tolerated it because I had no choice. Now that I have that choice, there's no going back for me.

My house is OK

During my husband's second visit to Metro Manila in 1994 (we were not yet married then), he was surprised to see a number of super-sized luxury hotels with enormous lobbies. As lobbies go, these hotels beat a large proportion of London hotels. While we were having a drink in the lobby of Edsa Shangri-La Hotel, there was an ensemble orchestra playing at one end and a rock band playing at the other end. They didn't get in each other's way. Due to the hotel's vastness and opulence, one could be forgiven for thinking they were in Hotel de Paris Monte Carlo, or in the Four Seasons hotel in New York. The truth was, they weren't. They were in a luxurious patch of Metro Manila.

On leaving the hotel, it isn't long before one notices smelly rivers choked by litter, heaps of garbage, the smell of urine in some areas, evidence of smog on building façades, and gasoline-scented air. There are a lot of these grubby patches intertwined with the luxury patches – a contrast that many don't see. When one is living in such an environment, these contrasts become part of everyday life and one becomes immune to them. The boundaries of these contrasts become blurry and the patches merely blend into one another. Philippines is not alone in having these contrasting patches. However, once again, compared to other countries I've lived in, the contrast between such patches in the Philippines is profoundly noticeable.

Let's talk about Maria, a hypothetical but typical Filipina. Maria owns a house into which she puts a great deal of effort to make it beautiful.

She drives an air-conditioned car so that she won't be breathing the smog on her way from home to work. Maria is quite happy driving through streets with litter as long as the traffic is not heavy on that day. The river beside where Maria works is smelly and much polluted but it doesn't matter because her workplace is air-conditioned, and has luxurious furnishings and well-manicured gardens. After work, Maria decides to meet up with friends at a nice restaurant in one of Philippine's modern shopping complexes. When Maria is back home, everything is nice and clean, so she's OK.

I was in one of those restaurants one day in 2013 and when I looked around, I felt a sudden pang of sadness. I saw many Marias around me. Together, we were happy inside that beautiful and clean restaurant. Sadly, we were oblivious to the contrasts around us outside.

There is more to those contrasts than merely aesthetics. It is cultural too. It appeared to me that everyone had their own bubble to protect them from the nasty outside elements. As long as their bubble followed them wherever they went, then life was OK and it didn't matter what it was like outside. There was a lack of national awareness that actually, each having their own bubble was not enough. Each of those Marias was not OK inside her house because outside, it was grubby, smelly and full of rubbish, and that had an indirect impact on everyone.

The culture of 'As long as my spaces are OK, whatever is outside my space doesn't matter' was with me while I was growing up. I too was once blind, which stopped me from blaming any of the Marias in that restaurant. The norms that one has grown up with are the true norms until one has been exposed to other places where the norms are different. I sympathise with the Marias who have already realised this problem but sadly, they account for just a few of the many other Marias out there. For the protection of those few Marias, they needed to travel in air-conditioned cars. For their sanity, they needed to make their homes beautiful and turn a blind eye to the rest. They had control inside their houses but mitigating the outside environment is almost an impossible task.

Whenever I went to the Philippines, I stayed in beautiful air-conditioned accommodation, travelled in air-conditioned cars and went to nice air-conditioned restaurants in nice areas to escape the patches I didn't want to be in. I made sure I had my bubble, and that was the sad truth - shame on me!

Blatant corruptions

Nineteen years after having left Philippines, blatant corruption pretty much still runs in the veins of the country.

Going back in history, at the top level, the world once saw *People Power* at work. That peaceful movement, backed by the people of the Philippines, led to the exile of the former dictator-president Ferdinand Marcos Sr. The Marcos family was reported to have stolen approximately £7bn from the Filipinos while the head of the family was in office. The aftermath of such corruption can still be seen in the large proportion of Filipinos still living in extreme poverty.

During my later visits there, it was still quite common to see politicians enjoying extravagant lifestyles after championing government projects, especially infrastructure projects 'worth' millions of pesos (so they say). Some Filipinos would defend this behaviour on the grounds that their favourite politicians had stolen less than other politicians.

Tragically, blatant corruption does extend to every level of society. I grew up seeing friends and extended family members placing bills in their driver's licence wallets, just in case they were caught breaching driving regulations by traffic officers. I witnessed many gifts given to corporate and government employees in exchange for favours. I heard about crimes or breaches in regulations that remained unchecked due to kickbacks. Falsification of documents was taken lightly by the general public. For example, there used to be a law that required every high school student to plant one hundred trees before they could graduate. As far as I know, many students graduated (including me) and yet, Philippines has never been swamped with trees.

To add another dimension, those who refused to engage in acts of corruption could sometimes be threatened by those who do. I know of someone close to me who suddenly needed to move after she received a death threat. She simply did not accept a bribe and that was enough to cause her to make a life-changing decision that she didn't really want to make.

I am very much aware that, so far, I haven't said anything about corruption that is not true outside of the Philippines. However, the scale of corruption is what makes Philippines different from the other countries I have lived in. The magnitude of what I am describing here can only be understood once someone has lived in my native country. In the Philippines, I could not live my life without witnessing acts of corruption most of the time. In the UK, I could live my life without witnessing acts of corruption most of the time. On the whole, that doesn't really make things better. However, it does help my sanity.

During my last visit to the Philippines, the amount of corruption I observed was about the same as when I left in 1995. However, I was definitely more sensitive and less tolerant to it due to the ways of living I have grown accustomed to in the UK. Unless I have no other choice, there is no reason for me to go back.

What's in a name?

I was born *Ivy Aurelio Laforteza*. In the Philippines, it is customary that when a woman marries, she drops her maiden middle name, makes her maiden surname her married middle name and adopts her husband's surname as her married surname. The children inherit their mother's married middle and last names. Let's say I got married to *Juan Santos*. My married name would be *Ivy Laforteza Santos*. If I had a daughter, she would be called *Maria Laforteza Santos*. If I had a son, he would be called *Mario Laforteza Santos*.

In the Philippines, I would have been legally identified as *Ivy Laforteza Santos* because that's what would have been written in my passport. In anywhere else in the world, I am legally identified as *Ging Aurelio Laforteza*. I changed my name by deed poll. The reason behind that is a long story and not really the focus of this book. The point is, I changed my name because I chose to, and I have the freedom and the right to do so − except in the Philippines.

Upon advice from the Philippine Embassy in Australia (I was living in Australia then), I needed to apply in person to the Philippine Consulate General in Manila to have my name changed. Even though I was told by the embassy that my wish was possible, the consulate in Manila declined my request in person. They stated that merely wanting to change a name is not valid grounds for changing that name. The only valid reasons are either divorce from or death of a husband. At that point, my husband and I talked about getting a divorce and then getting married again after I'd changed my name (*Wink!*).

I was surprised that the consulate advice was contradictory to what the embassy in Australia had told me. I was irritated because I had already spent money and had wasted so much effort preparing the supporting documents as per the embassy's advice. I was angry because my country was dictating who I was supposed to be. It's only a name but it's an important part of my identity.

When I told my big sister about this, she told me that her name includes 'Maria' because at that time, the Catholic Church would not baptise babies if their parents did not include names of saints in their babies' names. Thanks goodness I was born later when things had changed.

I love the fact that in the UK, I can choose whatever I want to call myself and not be forever governed by marriage conventions nor be at the mercy of sheer luck that the name my parents gave me is the one I would like to keep for life. Instead, my identity is defined by myself and me alone – not by my family, not by other people, not even by my husband, not by religion, and not by my country. I live with my choices and I like to keep it that way.

False helplessness

Although my desire to live permanently again in the Philippines constantly weakened with each passing year, I wasn't decided until my fifth trip in 2013/2014.

I was riding a taxi on my way back to my apartment one evening and unsurprisingly, I was stuck in a traffic jam. Although there was some movement (probably slower than 5mph), the vehicles were stationary most of the time. After a while, maybe an hour, an on-call ambulance pulled in from a side street and ended up next to my taxi.

I should have known but I didn't see it coming – no one gave way! Yes, we were stationary most of the time but there were movements too from time to time. If only everyone had been kind enough to pull over, the ambulance would have got through eventually ahead of everyone.

Instead, the ambulance was next to my taxi and travelled at the same pace for about forty-five minutes until the traffic eased.

I cannot help but imagine how dreadful the situation must have been inside that ambulance. I saw in my mind someone holding the hand of a dying patient they cared for very much and feeling helpless that the ambulance was going nowhere. Every second mattered and yet, time had stood still. I was upset and crying in sympathy because the situation should not have been helpless – if only people had given way! I was also crying because I imagined that that person inside the ambulance could have been me holding the hand of someone I cared for very much. Most likely, I would have felt helpless too.

After the traffic had cleared a little and the ambulance had been able to get through, I was able to compose myself and contemplate what had just happened. I concluded that if that scenario had actually happened to me and the person I cared for had died, I don't think I could ever have forgiven the society that had behaved in that way.

That experience was probably one of the most unforgettable moments in my life - for the wrong reasons. That evening, I decided that unless I am forced to (for whatever reason) and unless significant cultural changes happen, I would never live permanently in my own native country again. That night was the last straw.

Just minding my own business

I was born, raised, and grew up in a small town in the Philippines. It was a fun-filled childhood with a close-knit family and community. Everyone knew each other and everyone knew about everyone else's lives. There was camaraderie among neighbours and all the parents knew each other well. My siblings and I were able to play with our neighbours' kids any time without setting appointments, and we ate and watched TV at each other's homes without reservations. There was a very strong bond within the community. Kindness and concern for neighbours reigned, and everyone was willing to lend a hand to whoever needed help. Anyone could just knock on a door and borrow anything they needed, e.g., rice, salt, etc. Friends were regarded as family members, and our whole street celebrated Christmas and New Year with fireworks and simple meals.

I've now lived outside of the Philippines for almost twenty-eight years. Although my childhood is worth reminiscing about, life there no longer appears to be how it was. When I returned home for a short vacation, there was a huge gathering. These gatherings, attended by relatives and friends from everywhere, are a huge part of the Filipino culture. Nothing has changed in that respect. However, I noticed that the gathering did not focus only on having fun, and sharing adventures and experiences in life. It was also an avenue for comparing each other's status, successes and failures. It served as a tally board for competitions on who had the most successful children, the biggest house, the nicest cars, the most flourishing businesses, and many other similar topics. The unfortunate ones, who were considered as not meeting the general standard of success, were maligned, discriminated against, and even not recognised.

I realised I had changed. Casual conversations involving detailed descriptions of other people's lives were no longer pleasing to my ears, especially when they were about someone's life failures and shortcomings. It sounded like there was an element of gossiping in those conversations. Perhaps traditionally this was acceptable, but as I was not used to that type of conversation, I found it very unproductive and destructive. To me, those topics defeated the very essence of why my relatives and friends were at that gathering, especially when we all had just been to church. It was an experience that I learned from and accepted as part of my heritage, but it's something that I will not tolerate nor embrace.

Back to my present world outside of the Philippines, I can say that I am very much contented and happy knowing that I can live a life without judgement. The Western culture values privacy and although life is always busy, it is very productive. I prefer to see people in my circle supporting and building each other up, rather than pulling each other down. And I am happy to see the progress and financial successes of my friends and families.

GLH
Philippines to United States of America

12: My great rewards

My move from the Philippines to the United Kingdom was the beginning of what I consider my calling. There was a lot of pain at the start but the rewards that came later were far greater than those pains. This chapter describes the greatest rewards I have received from my first journey.

Multiple perspectives

I cannot describe the joy I feel every time I see AND feel more than one cultural perspective at the same time. It is similar to how I feel when a piece of music goes straight to my heart, or a shot of tequila goes straight to my head! Reading about other people's perspectives through books, magazines or museums just isn't the same as actually SEEING them and FEELING all the emotions that go with them.

For example, I grew up in the Philippines seeing police officers carrying guns and seeing armed security guards at building entrances. I also grew up in a gated community with 24-hour watch by private armed security personnel. Each of the houses in the gated community also had their own fences and lockable gates. Those were my norms before and the presence of armed guards made me feel secure.

When I arrived in the UK, it was very different. Police officers did not normally carry guns and if you saw them armed, it was certain that something seriously dangerous was happening. There were no armed guards in buildings either. Most houses did not have locked gates and strangers had direct access to their doorsteps. It was pretty odd at first but as years went by, they became my new normal. I felt secure because I didn't see guns.

When I went back to the Philippines and saw my old 'normal', I had goosebumps. I couldn't wait to be out of a bank because the sight of security guards with handguns/shotguns made me feel worried that something bad might happen at any time. I was shocked when I visited the university where I completed my first undergraduate degree because I was greeted by armed security guards who wanted to check my ID. I stayed in hotels guarded by armed security personnel. I felt uneasy.

When I've actually managed to detach myself from the scene to become merely an observer, I was in awe of my thoughts and emotions. I was able to give, at the same time, two interpretations of what I was seeing: one from a Filipino's point of view and the other from a Brit's point of view. It was as though I was two persons talking to each other and describing why certain things were happening in the way they happened, suggesting how things could happen, and predicting what was likely going to happen.

Having two cultural backgrounds also enables me to feel all the emotions associated with different perspectives. I believe this is the point where having the ability to observe one thing and to digest two different meanings at the same time becomes even richer. One can learn from other people's thoughts by reading their accounts. However, it is only through actual experiences that one can feel other people's emotions. When I saw security personnel carrying guns during my visit to the Philippines, I found it awesome that I felt safe and unsafe - at the same time.

Here's another example. One of my experiences in the UK that I contemplated for many years was the reaction I saw to the death of a loved one. A Brit I know, who I will refer to as Ben, was scheduled to go away on holiday for a month. Sadly, a few days before his departure, his father died a natural death.

Having known for a few years then that Brits' behaviours could be different from Filipinos', I was intrigued what Ben's response would be. If Ben had been a Filipino, I would have been one hundred per cent sure that he would have rescheduled his holiday for after the funeral. If Ben had had siblings abroad, I would have been ninety-five per cent sure too that his siblings would have flown back home from wherever they were in the world.

There is some unspoken expectation in Philippine society that immediate family members do not engage in leisure activities during a period of bereavement. In contrast, Ben decided to miss the funeral and go on holiday instead. I'm sure that many Brits would have rescheduled their holidays, but I'm also sure that many Brits would have gone away to engage in enjoyable activities only days after the death of a loved one. Either way, it would have been most likely that their relatives and friends wouldn't have had opinions about it.

At that time, I didn't criticise Ben's decision but I did not feel comfortable about it either. I started analysing what kind of child he was to his father that he was able to do what he did. Although he was closer to his mum, his relationship with his dad was a loving one. Based on what I had seen, Ben was caring towards his parents.

I cannot see any fault in what Ben did, but why then did I not feel comfortable? It took me a few years to conclude that the only answer lay in my mindset which was formed while growing up in the Philippines. It was a mindset that only knew a Philippine way of handling death or grief. My mind has expanded since then. I now see that we don't need to stop living our lives while grieving. Ben going to exotic places and engaging in fun activities is not a statement that Ben did not love nor care for his dad. Rather, it may simply be how he chose to deal with a sad circumstance in his life.

I feel rich and so privileged whenever I remember experiences such as the above two examples. The multiple perspective mind is what keeps me wanting to live in different places, and I am addicted to it.

Personal growth

I practise the philosophy of adopting and nurturing the good traits and ways of every culture, and dropping the bad traits and ways of those cultures. That way, I am hoping I will end up with the best of all worlds. It's logical, and doing so makes me less a Filipino over time and more a citizen of the world.

Sadly, I know that my philosophy draws criticism from many Filipinos. They will judge my transformations as trying to be 'different from them' (with a negative connotation), or as being snobbish about my roots (belittling my origin), or as feeling superior because I've lived abroad (colonial mentality). For some, it may also be seen as being ungrateful or disloyal to my native country. From where I stand, it is simply about one thing – personal growth. There is no progress if there is no acknowledgement that something is not right. There will be no growth if there is no willingness to change – for the better.

Looking back, one of the Filipino traits I would like to keep is the Filipino ability to express emotions with less inhibition than the British would. It's healthier and it makes people more human. Having said that though, I wouldn't like it taken to extremes either. One of the Filipino traits I would like to eliminate in me is the Filipinos' lack of integrity. Blatant corruptions exist in all levels of society and they cause a lot of self-inflicted sufferings among us.

On the other side, one of the British traits I would like to keep in me is the British passion for personal growth rather than for material things. They will spend more money and/or time learning something. I often say to others that if I were to compare two families of equal financial standing, one from the Philippines and the other from the UK, I would bet that the Filipino family would most likely have a much bigger and nicer house, and a flashier car (or cars). One of the British traits I would definitely not like to inherit is the British love for The Royal Family/Clan. I cannot see any point in the monarchy's existence in the 21st century. I certainly I cannot make sense why ordinary people (a substantial percentage of them cannot afford to buy their own houses) must pay towards the ultra-extravagant lifestyle of the royals (who are a billion times richer). There seem to be a national ignorance about where a percentage of the taxpayers' money go. Or worse, there seem to be a national justification for obliging ordinary people to pay towards the ultra-extravagant lifestyle of the Royal Family/Clan in exchange for a fairytale-like entertainment. Many Brits see elegance and nothing but cute princes and princesses when they look at The Royal Family/Clan. I, on the other hand, see the grave oppressions and sufferings the monarchy system brought to its colonies across the world in the past – all in the name of the 'great' British Empire! To my eyes, there is no elegance in there - only a glitzy fake one. Many Brits today fail to separate reality from fairytale, and to think rather than merely follow the herd like sheep.

I also realised that in order for me to feel at home in a country outside of Philippines, I needed to embrace both the good and the bad things about my new home. Embracing doesn't mean adopting the bad things but rather it's learning from the bad things and working around them.

As a general example, one thing that really irritated me before about the Brits was a lack of action when it comes to putting something right that is wrong. They rant at each other but those conversations usually ended with an 'oh well', meaning 'that's just how things are so we'll leave it at that'.

In the strictest sense, being a ranter is not necessarily bad; it depends on the context. However, from my viewpoint, the Brits' general level of ranting when compared with their general level of action is quite lopsided. So generally, I rate British ranting as 'bad'.

As a specific example, Brits will often talk about how appalling British customer service is. Sadly, only a very few will make efforts to challenge the service providers. As a result, the general standard of customer service in the UK remains appalling.

Over the years, I've learned to accept the ranting without getting irritated (embracing the 'bad' habit). Instead, I try to do something to alleviate the issue (work around it). I have written many complaint letters to senior managers, directors and CEOs of companies. There were hits and misses but I am hoping that generally, my complaints were helpful. I submitted those complaints not just for myself but also for the general public.

If I had stayed in the Philippines all my life, I am unsure whether I would have had the nerve to talk to executive officers of big companies on an equal footing. I suspect that I would have remained under the spell of a very hierarchical society. Today in the UK, I consider my feeling of empowerment to do something for the greater good as one of my personal growths.

Lastly, one of the most valued experiences of personal growth I have experienced while living in the UK is the reconfirmation that self-worth must come from within rather than be concocted artificially by outside forces.

In Philippine culture, a person's job is a reflection of themselves. I've been told that this was also pretty much true in British culture. However, due to some changes in the mindset in recent decades, many Brits now consider their jobs as something they merely do to suit their circumstances; be it for reasons of personal interest, convenience to suit their family's lifestyle, or as means to support their other pursuits.

It is very common for Filipinos with well-established careers in the Philippines to hold jobs that are well below their qualifications at the start of their journeys overseas. That doesn't mean that Filipinos are less capable or less intelligent. A lot of times, this is merely due to Philippine credentials not being recognised internationally. Hence, Filipinos overseas often need to prove themselves first before they arrive at where they should have started in the first place.

Since Filipinos would consider their jobs as a reflection of who they are, many Filipino immigrants would feel embarrassed about having jobs overseas that they would consider inferior to what they might have had at home. Unfortunately, this feeling creates a lot of other problems, setting in motion, a vicious circle. I know of someone who used to be a managing director of a small company in the Philippines who became a janitor overseas. He didn't take it very well. His self-belief dwindled and eventually, he suffered from depression.

On the other hand, many Brits would consider the circumstance of having an 'inferior' job as only temporary. It's merely a state they are in, rather than a definition of who or what they are capable of. They may hate what they do under those unfavourable circumstances, but they would be less likely to think they are inferior to what they were before circumstances led them to their new jobs.

I have so many friends in the UK who were once shop assistants, taxi drivers, baristas, cleaners, cargo men, waiters, etc, while pursuing their careers. For example, I have a friend who was a part-time lecturer and part-time grocery store assistant at the same time. Obviously, her students would see her at the shop, but it was no big deal. I was once a lecturer in Manila and I could not really see myself doing something similar there without my story going viral. Another friend was a professional photographer and cleaner. Both friends talked openly about their experiences without a trace of embarrassment.

Life is challenging and sometimes, we need to do things that we would rather choose not to do. As long as we're not causing any harm to others, what is there to feel ashamed of? I know, it is more easily said than done. However, one lesson I have learned in the UK is to recognise that whatever my job is, as long as it's decent, it is not a measure of my worth.

Losing vs gaining identity

'Losing identity' is the phrase I more commonly come across rather than 'gaining identity'.

More often than not, the articles I've read describe how Filipinos found themselves 'lost' because they had adopted different ways outside of the Philippines; philosophies and values different from those in the Philippines. This seems to say that although they've been removed physically from the Philippines for a period of time, the anchor of their being Filipino has remained substantially strong. Hence, they feel that they've lost a part of themselves when they realise that those Filipino parts are no longer there. Some people even feel guilty about betraying or being ungrateful to the Philippines. I've also heard that many immigrants from other countries also experience this issue of losing their identities.

To me, my incredible journey has enabled me to <u>gain</u> my identity, not lose it. I saw many perspectives that were different from those I grew up with, and I adopted them once I was convinced it was right to do so. I am no longer bound by any specific culture, religion, family traditions, national protocols, or societal expectations. What I believe and practise are my choices, which enforce who I truly am. I welcome the changes in me rather than feel sorry for what has changed in me. I look forward to continue changing during my journey and who I become each day is defined by myself.

It is indeed my wish to be not merely a citizen of a country, but rather a citizen of the world.

13: My take on this

I am truly very grateful for my journeys across a few cultures. My path was very rocky to begin with but it led me to a few destinations that introduced me to different worlds. I had no idea that my move from the Philippines to the United Kingdom would give me the chance to evolve from a naïve third-world creature (as my cousin would say) to someone who has some awareness of what it's actually like in other worlds.

The journey was an extremely valuable education for me, and one that has changed my many views about life. It has changed me – a lot. I consider my transformations priceless and, although impossible, I would love to keep on moving from one country to another until the end of my life.

Of all the things that I have learned, there is one general principle that I value the most and have followed during successive moves: adopt the positive traits of a culture and drop its negative traits. If a person keeps on doing that while moving from one country to another, I believe that person becomes better each time.

A friend once asked me, 'With all the moves, with which country does your loyalty lie?' My answer was *to the world.*

I do sometimes wonder what the world would be like if everyone's loyalty was to the world and there was no *us* or *them*.....

I wish I had read a book like this one ahead of my first journey to give me an idea of what lay ahead across the globe. I am hoping that through this book, people who have already moved and are currently having difficult adjustment periods may take comfort that their experiences and the whole range of emotions they're feeling right now are not unique to them. I am also hoping that through this book, people who are still considering whether to move or not may find my experiences worthy of reflection before they begin their own journeys.

Many people will agree with me that every country in the world has its own beauty and shortcomings. A place can only be good or bad depending on how one looks at it. It's like dating: the country and the person must have matching personalities. The poorest country in the world can be seen as attractive to someone who lives to help others.

During the early adjustment period, it may not be instantly obvious whether your personality suits your new country. I know some people who moved from the Philippines and, after a year, they went back. I was surprised because their personalities seemed suited to the UK. I'm sure that they had good reasons for moving back but I am also sure that if only they had stayed longer, chances are, they would have found a home in the UK.

Whatever was desirable to you before can become undesirable over time, and vice versa. I lost track counting the number of stories about Filipinos going back to the Philippines to live there permanently again, only to find out that they felt like strangers in their own country after moving back. I can easily imagine that. People do change so when you leave, there's no going back to exactly the same you again. As I said earlier, I've changed a lot and I am now more British than Filipino.

Your experiences during your adjustment period will differ from others'. However, the principle is the same. The adjustment period is merely a process that you have to go through. It all might feel extremely difficult but chances are, there is nothing wrong with you. You're simply inside a cultural void and learning from your new environment - just like you did when you were a child. However, unlike a child who has a blank canvas concept of the world, you already have formed your own truths. Suddenly finding yourself in a world with a different set of truths can be intimidating, and your attitude will play a major role in the outcome. Some people will pack their bags, others will stay and sulk, while others will cherish their transformative moments in their new homes.

To those of you who are finding their adjustment periods extremely difficult, I really believe that as each day passes by, the difficulties will lessen, if not totally disappear. Some of my difficulties went away by doing nothing and some merely through long exposure to my new environment. As soon as those difficulties were gone, I regained a bit more headspace to tackle the rest of my other difficulties.

I hope that this book helps you. I believe that I haven't said anything here that has overwhelming wisdom. I am hoping, however, that by simply sharing my experiences, you will take comfort that whatever darkness you're currently experiencing, that darkness is not unique to you. I hope, in knowing that, you will find the strength to overcome your adjustment period so that you can eventually receive your rewards for taking such a bold step to widen your horizon.

14: epilogue: a small fish

Someone asked me some time ago what I'd rather be: a small fish in a big pond, or a big fish in a small pond. Without a doubt, I would choose being a small fish in a big pond. For me, it's about growing continuously and having the space to grow into.

People who know me well would know that I am always trying something new. I am like a cat. Sometimes, my curiosity gets the better of me; sometimes, it gets me to rewarding spots many can only imagine.

I don't think I can actually become a big fish in a small pond. Why? As soon as I get big enough and my pond gets small enough, I jump to another pond – a bigger one. I welcome each jump and look forward with great enthusiasm to new things that constantly make me change and grow.

Upon news of my move (again) to another country, a good friend once looked into my eyes and very sadly told me that he wished I would soon find what I was looking for. I appreciated his good wishes for me as I felt that his heart was in the right place. However, he was wrong about the reason why I kept on moving. I had already found what I was looking for, a long time ago. I am an explorer of cultures and collecting new experiences to gain insights from many perspectives is what my life is about. Moving from one place to another is not my way of escaping life, but rather, it is my life.

Not all who wander are lost. They may merely prefer to remain a small fish.

Appendix

Our cleaner drove a Mercedes Benz

One day, our cleaner parked her car next to ours on the street in front of our house. She had a big, white, shiny Merc (as they call Benz cars in the UK) while ours was a compact, tatty-looking white car; the brand and model I can't even remember because it was so forgettable. We called our car Clunky, as the name pretty much described her.

That scenario would have seemed bizarre in the Philippines. I found out later that day that our cleaner's boyfriend owned the Merc. Still, it was strange to me because in the Philippines, no cleaner drives a Mercedes Benz. I wish I'd asked her to give me a ride. Not everybody has the chance of having a ride in his or her cleaner's Merc. ☺

I pointed with my mouth

Brits point to things with their fingers. Filipinos point to things with their fingers or mouths. It is a common gesture in the Philippines to point with one's mouth. We do this by puckering our lips, and moving our heads in the direction of the object while further extending our lips towards it.

If you're not Filipino, remember that when you see this, it is not an invitation to a kiss!

Narrow panties please

In the UK, getting clothes small enough to fit me is a nightmare. Getting panties that fit me was even harder during my early years here.

Panties in the UK all had wide crotches which caused me to develop irritations (itchiness, redness and mild pain) in my groin area where it meets my legs. I bought a number of different brands yet nothing suited me. I didn't have this problem in the Philippines and I wondered what the cause of the problem might be. ☺ (Wink! Wink!)

To my great relief, since around 2015, I can now wear one style of Marks & Spencer panties that are problem-free. The question is, has my body changed? (Answer: No, it hasn't!)

No nice hats for me

I'd never worn a hat before I came to live in the UK because during my time in the Philippines, hats were not common then. In the UK, I like seeing ladies wearing hats so during my second winter, I thought I'd wear one too.

I bought a nice cloche hat to go with my work clothes. The day I wore it for the first time, was the day I looked like a tabletop! I was so pleased walking to work with my lovely hat but when I removed it, my hair was squashed and my fringe (or bangs as we say in the Philippines) was glued to my forehead. I rushed to the toilet to wet my hair hoping that, once dried, the bounce would come back. It didn't! My options were, to continue wearing my hat in the office and look weird, or to take off my hat and sell my tabletop look as a new fashion trend!

Since then, I only wear hats when I don't care how I look, and when my hair is tied so it doesn't really matter if it doesn't bounce back. A few years after, I learned that other Filipino women in the UK experienced the same. Sounds like Asian hair is less bouncy!

Chip and Dale

Chippendale furniture in the UK has a following. The pieces are usually of Georgian, rococo, or neoclassical style, and are named after Thomas Chippendale, a British cabinetmaker in London in the eighteenth century. Current values vary from less than £1,000 to more than £1m per item. I didn't know that before.

My husband and I met with friends one evening and the host presented a couple of chairs. The crowd was impressed because the chairs were genuine heritage chairs. I was puzzled though. I stared and scrutinised carefully all the parts of the chairs, which were about four metres away from where I sat. I swear they were identical. After it became obvious to me that I was the only one not acquainted with the chairs, I asked,

'Which one is Chip and which one is Dale?' The room was filled with laughter. I realised then that I needed a pair of hearing aids. 😊

More preservatifs please

It was our honeymoon and we went for a one-day boat cruise on Lake Leman from Geneva to Montreux. While on the outdoor deck, we fancied some scones and coffee so my husband requested some from one of the crew. Our order arrived but we didn't realise until after the staff had gone that there was not enough jam for piggies like us. We waited for a while but no one came back so I volunteered to go in to ask for some more.

On my way to the café, I remembered that people in Geneva speak French. I also thought that they would be more helpful to visitors who tried to speak their language, no matter how badly. I made an effort to speak French. *Preserves*, the generic UK term for jam/marmalade, came into my mind. I also thought that many French words ended in *tif* so maybe the French for strawberry jam, I thought, would be *preservatif*.

Halfway down to the café, I saw a member of the crew. I enthusiastically said, '*Bonjour*, could I please have some *preservatif*?" He looked shocked and said, 'No, no, no, pharmacy, pharmacy!' I was puzzled, of course. I mimicked the movements of scooping jam from a jar and placing the jam in my mouth. I also closed my eyes and made some sound to create that 'yummy, yummy' impression. He looked even more shocked and he kept on shaking his head.

His colleague passed by and he said something to her, in French of course. I told her that I wanted some more *preservatif*. I also made an even bigger gesture of placing an invisible amount of jam into my mouth and licked my lips to relay that strawberry jam is yummy. She too, looked shocked and told me to go to the pharmacy. At that point, I decided to get some more jam myself from the café. I did, and my husband and I enjoyed our afternoon tea on the outer deck while cruising along the lake.

At the end of our one-day lake cruise, we decided to walk back to our hotel. We were happily chatting when a poster at a bus stop we passed caught my attention. On the poster was the word *Preservatif* in big, bold, orange letters. Below the word was an image of what a *preservatif* actually is. It was not strawberry jam – it was a condom!

Printed in Great Britain
by Amazon